SOUTHWEST WISCONSIN LIBRARY SYSTEM

W9-AUY-591

3 9696 00458 8832

Oct '91

639.9
Ure

Ure, Jim
Hawks and Roses /

DATE DUE

NO 22 '91		
JA 26 '93	JAN 2 4 2002	
MR 30 '93	MAY 3 0 2002	
NO 2 '93		
DE 1 '93	FEB 2 2 2005	
FE 27 '95	DEC 1 7 2005	
AP 21 '95		
FE 05 '96		
MY 17 '96		
MR 6 '9		
NOV 2 8 2000		

WITHDRAWN

DODGEVILLE PUBLIC LIBRARY
139 S. Iowa St.
Dodgeville, WI 53533

HAWKS AND ROSES

Also by

Jim Ure

*Bait for Trout: Being the Confessions
of an Unorthodox Angler*

DODGEVILLE PUBLIC LIBRARY
139 S. Iowa St.
Dodgeville, WI 53533

HAWKS
AND ROSES

Jim Ure

DODGEVILLE PUBLIC LIBRARY
139 S. Iowa St.
Dodgeville, WI 53533

First edition
93 92 91   5 4 3 2 1

Copyright © 1991 by Jim Ure

All rights reserved. No part of this book may be
reproduced in any manner whatsoever without
written permission from the publisher.

This is a Peregrine Smith Book, published by
Gibbs Smith, Publisher
P.O. Box 667
Layton, Utah 84041

Design by Mary Ellen Thompson
Manufactured in the United States of America

Library of Congress Cataloging-in-Publication Data

Ure, Jim, 1939-
        Hawks and roses / Jim Ure.
            p.   cm.
        Includes bibliographical references.
        ISBN 0-87905-373-9
        1. Birds of prey--Utah. 2. Wildlife rescue--Utah. 3. Ure, Jim,
1939-   4. Bird watchers--Utah--Biography. I. Title.
QL696.F3U73 1991
639.9 ' 789 ' 092--dc20
[B]   90-49741
                                                                  CIP

To Stellanie, Corydon and Matthew.
What roads we have traveled.

Preface

I am frequently asked, "What good are birds of prey?" This seems a logical question, since human beings' homocentricity has provided a long-running rationale for their dominion over all things going back as far as the development of agriculture and the domestication of livestock. At one time modern man may have lived in an easy partnership with Gaea, the earth mother, but this seems to have long ago been lost as he exerted his need to have the world on his terms, rather than vice versa. What good is it? How can we make it work for us?

We have become accustomed to applied research that solves our problems, and to science providing us with a vast array of cures and comforts; this has shaped our view that everything, in some way, must benefit the human species. Yet I rankle at the question, often answering with a question posed by one of those Johnny-come-lately, smarty-pants naturalists: "What good are you?"

We're all on this earth together, and if any inventory of goodness is taken by the heavenly hosts, humans may be the animals in danger of being condemned to dance an eternal quickstep on the hot stones of hell's ballroom.

But let's set judgments aside: humanity just *is*, with all its head-scratching foibles. Hawk just *is*. When we get to know hawk better (and we will; animal communication is in its infancy), we may scratch our heads over bird's peccadilloes. Birds of prey are neither good nor bad by some human definition. They just do their bird thing, and in the process thrill us with their beauty and the way they live. They are very important because *nothing* is a bird of prey like a bird of prey. That's what they do best, and that's why they are good.

We recognize something wonderful and uplifting in birds of prey, and like art galleries or symphonies, they contribute to our mental health and tranquillity, all of which seem to be in diminishing supply as we near the end of the twentieth century.

Have they contributed to homo sapiens' security as a species?

Certainly birds of prey are important to the earth's equilibrium. They eat oodles of mice and other rodents, and if we still insist on knowing how they benefit us, they are telling us more and more about what may cause problems in human diet and environment, since they are sensitive barometers at the top of the food chain. Yesterday the peregrine falcon's eggs were important aids to discovering the dangers of DDT to humans and the environment; today birds of prey are telling us about DDT and other pesticides still being used in Mexico and Central America, the source of 40 percent of North America's vegetables.

My interest in birds began when I was very young. Growing up as a westerner, I was expected to be a hunter, and I readily related to birds of prey, most especially after I took up falconry. As a journalist after college, I wrote about natural history subjects and birds of prey whenever possible.

After marriage and the birth of my sons, the return to involvement through the rehabilitation of hawks, eagles, falcons and owls forced a reexamination of my relationship with my fellow creatures. The art of falconry, for instance, created conflicts for me when young birds were taken from the wild at a time when we—for all of us in the family worked very hard at this—were striving mightily to release birds of the same species so they could be free.

And the resolution of the internal conflicts over my own predatory feelings? I finally accepted these feelings. Predation is the way the world gets fed, and in the final analysis, something must die in order for everything to eat and live, vegetarians included. Predators just happen to go about food gathering directly and spectacularly; the rest of us get and eat our food without quite that drama.

This is the story of the relationship between my family—myself, my wife Stellanie, and our sons, Corydon and Matthew—and birds of prey during nearly fifteen years of "the project." Three thousand birds later, I look back and see that raptors taught us so much: that death is the shadow of life, giving us the necessary symmetry for a balanced, complexly simple earth; that sweetness especially comes from measuring against harshness—yin and yang; thesis, antithesis. Best of all, we learned to accept Gaea on her terms.

In return we tried to give back to the earth something of our labors and love, a meager gift perhaps, but it sounded like music to us.

Jim Ure
Holladay, Utah
1990

ACKNOWLEDGMENTS

I thank Stellanie Soter Ure, whose knowledge of hawks quickly surpassed my own, for an exciting and interesting life that enriched me in so many ways as we strode through those days of abundance. She provided me with scrupulously kept data from her records so I could match them with my own notebooks to accurately reconstruct certain events. Her editing and word-processing services were invaluable.

Cory and Matthew Ure provided me with additional information, especially recollections of certain birds—Chiquita, Homer, and Charles Lindberg the Lone Owl.

The origins of my life with birds began with my late father, whom I missed more than ever as I put this story together, and Dr. William H. Behle, Utah's renowned ornithologist and my mentor in bird matters at the University of Utah and later.

To my brother Joe, thanks for hard work and construction advice. Certain neighbors need kudos, including Dave and Mary Anne Keyser and their kids, Chris, Tony and Elizabeth; Ted and Joan Hansell; the late Frank and June Daughters; Rich McClure and Helen McClure; Hal Cannon; Jon Larson. Appreciation also goes to Madge Baird and Barbara Bannon, whose suggestions and edits improved this book significantly.

I cannot say enough about the friendship and education provided by Steve Chindgren, who also served as my falconry master. Other falconers who provided help include Dale Kessimakis, Terry Roundy, Roger Herron, Mike Bradford, Ron Roach, Ron Rollins, Charles Schwartz, Pat Benson, Ron Clarke, Steve Platt, Jim Hatchett, Gerald Richards, Joe Terry, Howard Brinkerhoff, Dino Newbold, Carel Brest van Kempen, Steve Tait and, of course, "The Grand Master," Morlan Nelson.

Special thanks to Ray Linder, friend, confidante, former president of the California Hawking Club. We laugh a lot when we're together and his information is good.

Some fellow rehabilitators with whom Stellanie shared knowledge and experience are the late Shawn Ogburn; Kathy Smith, now of Los Angeles (beloved sister and "thea"), and Hope Carpenter of Pennsylvania, among several others.

Information came from many sources, but particularly helpful with golden eagle data were Joe Murphy and Pat Benson. David Ellis's work was also helpful, as was that of the late Leslie Brown.

For information on large falcons, I am especially indebted to Steve Chindgren, Terry Roundy, and Clayton S. White, whose work in taxonomy is so highly regarded; for marsh hawks, Patricia Thompson and Frances Hammerstrom; for Harris' hawks, Bill Mader and the work of James C. Bednarz; for goshawks, Jessie Woody and Scott Nichols, now of Boise, our former neighbor whom we watched grow up, ever holding a hawk on his fist; and for Cooper's hawks, Carel Brest van Kempen. Thanks also go to Dee Porter for his willingness to fill in the blanks in my knowledge of the politics and natural history of Utah peregrines; to Carl Marti for his owl information; to the works of Beebe and Webster, McElroy, Mavrogordato, Amadon and Brown and, of course, Bent and Frederick II.

Efforts of government workers too often go unpraised. Many thanks to Harry Stiles, Dean Spackman, Susan McLane, Jim Hogue, Lucinda Schroeder, Terry Grosz, Bob Walters, Bob Hasenyager, Rick Schultz, Bernadette Hilbourn, Jim Guymon, Kevin Cherry, Mike Coffeen, and the Johnsons—Auston, Mike and Bruce. Appreciation must go to Don Paul, Angie Fleck, and, of course, Al and Ruth Heggen, Phil Wagner, and John Nagel (the latter two are now with Ducks Unlimited).

And bouquets to Dave Hall and Owen and Mary Ellen Hogle for their support, to Bruce Clements for a lot of legwork, and to my friend Jim Woolf, whose knowledge of "LBBs" helped me to grow and expand my knowledge in areas I might otherwise never have explored.

INTRODUCTION

Sunday evening, late February. The Promontory Mountains. I am looking for ferruginous hawks. They seem to be growing fewer in number. The big buteos should be drifting back now after luxuriating in the warmth of Arizona and southern Utah. The smart ones are still there, I think, stamping my feet in the shadow-blue snow in an attempt to warm them. My breath fogs the binoculars as I scan a ridge touched violet and peach by the light of the setting sun.

An adult golden eagle flies just above the ridge; it is a peculiar, scalloped flight. At the apogee of each scallop, she lifts just above the ridge to scan the sagebrush flats that fall from the foothills of the Promontory range into the vastness of Great Salt Lake. She drops below the ridge line, reappears, then drops again.

As the ridge runs out of itself and molds into the valley floor, she zips into a stringer of pinion and juniper that fingers into the sagebrush. Low in the stubby trees, she heads directly for a water-cut gulch, dropping into it, flying powerfully and purposefully. She is out of sight now. My eyes move down the gulch which passes next to an abandoned alfalfa field.

The eagle suddenly pops out of the gulch at full speed, rolling almost on her back as she plunges into the low growth. Through the glasses I can see snow being tossed up in a struggle.

Later I walk to the site. Between my rubberized toes in the snow, I see blood and bits of jackrabbit fur and the print of an eagle foot that measures ten inches. She's as big an eagle as any of the hundreds we held at our home.

Being part of a bird-of-prey rehabilitation project has been most enlightening, and I muse at what I have seen and learned: that hawks will drink water poured from a glass; that birds take exception to individual humans; that hawks and eagles will play with sticks and splash in water just for fun; that a hawk will follow a child to the bus stop; that mice loose in the house will eat cocoa and lima beans. I have learned that hawks, eagles and some owls can seem to care deeply for humans, and vice versa.

As I walk through the sage in the starlight, I retrace the eagle's flight path, realizing she had planned a sneak attack based on experience collected through many years of successful living. No longer surprised at the sentience of birds of prey, I inhale the frosty air that numbs the bridge of my nose. A balm of sage vapors, irrepressible even in the chill, wafts into my nostrils to comfort and warm me with its sweet familiarity as I crunch through the snow toward the distant truck.

The last flicker of sunlight illuminates two separate specks of rubble miles away in the vastness of Great Salt Lake: my spotting scope reveals the first to be Duckville Gun Club, its roof tilted at a crazy angle, the building smashed and tossed like a war victim, its entrails of beds and kitchenware and tiles and siding spilling onto the slowly receding mud flats. The second was once the headquarters of the U.S. Fish and Wildlife Service at Bear River Bay, where buildings and observation towers were scythed down by the same action—a sheet of pack ice pushed across the brackish bay by a strong northerly wind one bitter February night.

It's ironical that now the lake is dropping, sucked down by man-made pumps and light winters. It seems like just yesterday that the lake was at flood stage and we were waving good-bye to so many birds that had been part of our lives. Could the eagle I had just watched have been one of "ours," released from the old hacking station?

Lowering the scope, I am stunned by the devastation, yet comforted and humbled to know that destruction is the beginning of creation, and that the perpetual changes of nature have been observed by the wise eyes of eagles since the Eocene epoch seventy-five million years ago.

Big, open country. Releasing a golden eagle, Lakeside Mountains, Utah. (Photo Stellanie Ure)

1
THE MOUNTAIN WEST

> *Land is immortal, for it*
> *harbors the mysteries of*
> *creation.*
>
> —ANWAR SADAT

Nature writers wrestle with "a sense of place," since it tends to dictate who they are. I envy those who let the ocean define their writing, or a certain mountain range, or the saguaro desert. It seems so tidy, so focused to be able to say the Great Basin is what shaped this story, though it is really not quite so simple.

Our raptor activities extended to the corners of the very diverse Mountain West, reaching northwest to Boise, east to the Colorado border, west to the ghost towns of central Nevada, south to the bizarre glitter of Las Vegas. The events dictated the playing field, and for a significant portion of the life of my family, rubbed off on us and shaped us. (Chemically I am certain my kids are a confounding mélange of sage, sharp-shinned shit, lodgepole pine, Great Salt Lake water and equal parts basalt and Wingate sandstone. Oh yes, and gold, and trumpet-valve oil.)

On any spring day within this vast region, a peregrine can be brooding her eggs in a snowstorm in the Sawtooth Mountains of Idaho, while great horned owlets learn to fly in the hundred-degree heat of a cottonwood bottom near Lake Powell. It is an area of 230,000 square miles that ranges in elevation from 13,000-foot peaks to Sonoran landscapes less than 2,000 feet above sea level. At its heart is the Great Basin, the ocean-evoking vastness of peaks and troughs between the Wasatch Mountains and the Sierra Nevada. The basalt caps of Idaho and the deeply cut sandstone canyons of the Colorado Plateau bookend the basin.

While most of this land is arid, the irony is that its rivers are grand: the Green, the Colorado, the Snake. Its largest body of water, Great Salt Lake, provides no succor for agriculture (yet supports an abundance of life in its waters and at its margins).

Place names are its human history: Shoshone, Blackfoot, Winnemucca, Arapahoe, Meeteetse, Escalante, Fort Bridger, Fort Robidoux, Madison, Jefferson, Fremont, Gunnison, Carson, Soda Springs, Custer, Farmington, Bountiful, Silver City, Ophir, Carbon, Irontown, Dugway Proving Grounds, Electric Lake, Hill Air Force Base and the Idaho National Engineering Lab, formerly the National Reactor Testing Station.

This space is as big as the combined states of Maine, New Hampshire, Vermont, Massachusetts, Rhode Island, Connecticut, New York, New Jersey, Delaware, Pennsylvania, Maryland, Virginia and most of West Virginia. Westerners have become used to traveling these vast distances. Six hundred miles for a weekend of birding, fishing, or visiting far-flung relatives is a matter of routine.

Aside from a hundred-mile-long sliver of heavily populated land along the foot of the Wasatch Mountains in Utah, the communities are about sixty miles apart, each an hour by automobile on the soulless freeways, a little longer on the friendly state and county roads. We seldom need highway maps, for we are blessed with great vistas and the knowledge of how to get "there" passed on by anyone you care to ask.

We do, however, rely heavily on Bureau of Land Management and United States Geological Survey maps that define the economy, the recreation and the wildlife of the West by delineating land-use patterns—private ownership, federal land, mining claims, state land, national forest, wildlife refuges, state and national parks, Indian and military reservations. These boundaries are the source of much of western politics, but that is another book.

Land was what attracted the original settlers to the West. They brought with them an ethic that gave human beings domain over all. They dammed the rivers, killed the predators, tore out the sagebrush, grazed off the grass and then, after more than a hundred years, many looked back to mourn the lost innocence, the expired frontier.

The West we are part of is beginning to awaken slowly to the need to maintain a healthy balance between economics and our mother earth. This is the story of a small contribution made to conservation, assisted by many concerned westerners who brought thousands of hawks and eagles into our lives and hands from the far-flung reaches of the Mountain West.

A child's fascination with a hawk. Matthew Ure is counseled by a kestrel. (Photo by Stellanie Ure)

2
A Passion For Birds

Boys throw stones at frogs in sport;
frogs die in earnest.

—Plutarch

Birds had become a conscious part of my life by age six. So had a conservation ethic, although I had to kill a great many birds before the ethic became comfortably seated in the matrix of my experience.

My fascination with birds was developed by my father in a hothouse of natural history anecdotes. Dad had been immobilized by polio when he was three. To divert him, his parents would place a blanket next to the stream at their summer home in Ogden Canyon, where he spent hours watching kingfishers, soaring hawks, phoebes, otters and trout tailing in the clear water of the stream. He supplemented his observation with reading, and in the 1930s he worked several seasons in Yellowstone with the old Bureau of Fisheries.

Mother, on the other hand, admitted she was a nature naïf. She was athletic, a tennis and softball player, and met my father over the telephone (she was working as a draft-board clerk just as World War II was heating up). A couple of years later this improbable duo was married in spite of the warnings and concerns of relatives. Four children were born during the next thirteen years. I was first, followed by a sister, then two brothers. The marriage lasted more than fifty years, until my father's death in 1989.

We lived in what I call the "rurbs," neither rural nor suburb, a small island of development surrounded by farms in the Millcreek area of Salt Lake County. There were orchards and fields, and sparkling trout streams cascading from the nearby mouths of Millcreek and Big Cottonwood canyons; it was an idyllic place for a boy with a bent for nature.

Unable to take me to the fields and streams, Father instead encouraged my interest in natural history through storytelling and by introducing certain books. His stories of osprey and trout when he had worked in Yellowstone in the early 1930s held me spell-bound.

I remember sitting at the kitchen table in the bright Saturday morning sun. His breakfast of cucumbers, toast and onions—always liberally sprinkled with Tabasco—was finished, and Dad opened a book for a reading from Ernest Thompson Seton: ". . . for it was spring, and no wild thing should be hunted in spring," he read. This is my earliest recollection of a lesson in conservation.

Dad had hunted and fished a little in spite of his handicap. His heritage carried a nineteenth-century belief that hunting and fishing were manly and appropriate, although it would be years before I realized how it grieved him when something was actually killed. Mother was delighted when there was something new for the pot, so manly I decided to be.

For my seventh Christmas my parents gave me "the Bird Book." This was *Birds of America*, the classic 1917 work, updated in 1936, by T. Gilbert Pearson and John Burroughs, et al. It was the only bird book of consequence available to me since our local library system was always financially pinched. I read this book so thoroughly that its binding became loose, its plates smudged, its margins marked and annotated. The birds took me to their habitats—the eastern woods, the Pacific coast, the high plains. I learned of lands I could not find on maps (Keewatin, Ungava), and of distant places I would later recognize in different contexts (the Falklands, Angola). A housebound child could quickly forget the confining disciplines of his life in the fragrant pages of the Bird Book.

Savoring the color plates by Louis Agassiz Fuertes, I was flooded with strange and lovely yearnings as I studied pintails skimming a marsh at dawn. A peregrine pluming a meadowlark sent a chill of adventure through my scalp. Tears came when I read of the passenger pigeon and the heath hen, and wondered how human beings could ever become so greedy that they could destroy a beautiful species altogether. Gone forever, just like *my own death*. Extinction became an emotional, highly charged word for me.

To draw a bird was to *hold it*, so I copied the bird paintings and sketches endlessly, becoming fairly proficient. I believe it was an attempt to capture the freedom represented by the bird and its power of flight. (Perhaps this desire is what motivated the cave painter at Lascaux.) For a youngster whose father could not take him afield, drawing birds was the closest substitution possible. Besides, birds were pretty.

If only I could have a bird, perhaps to share its qualities and get to know it. Such a longing resulted in a certain amount of wildlife vandalism. I took two fledgling warblers from a nest in a tree near my grandmother's, thinking to raise them (I already had some vague ideas about falconry). They escaped my small box, and my grandmother later found the tiny corpses where they had hidden in dark corners on the top shelves of her storeroom. When questioned, I could not bring myself to tell how they had found their way into the house.

I felt deep remorse. Later, as hunting birds with slingshot and BB gun became sport, I found my triumphs ambivalently tinged with guilt. I would hold the small, still-warm body of a bird, fingering its lovely feathers, and wonder why I had killed it. Maybe these feelings are not so different from what the mourning human feels for the lost wilderness after he has tamed it with dams, timbering, and agriculture.

Trying to resurrect my victims, I took up taxidermy (with the help of a correspondence course from the Northwest School of Taxidermy in Omaha, Nebraska), and my basement room was filled with borax, bits of wire, glass eyes, Excelsior, surgical tools and the aroma of decomposing flesh. My finest works were a Bohemian waxwing and an eight-inch yellow perch.

I had to possess these creatures, in spite of my father's stern warning about game laws and killing "only what you eat." As self-punishment, I ate robins, English sparrows, and evening grosbeaks, usually cooked, if that is the word, on a stick over an open fire. Once I cooked a blue grouse in a friend's coal furnace. Another time another friend failed to gut our quail before cooking it. It was years before I could enjoy well-prepared game.

On a winter day when I was in fourth grade, two men from the local aviary unexpectedly came to my elementary school to present a lecture on falconry. While one talked, the other simply held a long-legged, noisy, black-and-white bird of prey with a crest. The demonstration bird was an Audubon's caracara (which many years later I learned was used to hawk rabbits by one of the men). This event inflamed my desire to have a hawk, and for several days I looked up the phone number of the aviary, then slammed the book closed in fear of the responding voice on the other end. What if the man hung up on me? What if he rebuffed me? Could I be too young? What if he simply said "no" to my one and only chance at a hawk? I knew of no other person in the world with an interest in hawks.

At last I worked up the courage to call. "I'd like to get a sparrow hawk," I said in my best Child Sincerely Yearning voice. I hardly dared suggest it, but did they have an extra one around I could buy? There would be the problem of getting the money, but children are great manipulators when they want something really badly.

"You'll have to catch one," said the keeper in a not-unkindly way. I drooped as a whole new set of problems confronted me. "Look at the big, dead cottonwood trees for woodpecker holes. Watch the adults go in the hole with food for the babies. Then climb up and take a baby."

Not even certain what a cottonwood tree was, I gulped, thanked him, and not daring to ask more, hung up, still longing for a sparrow hawk.

The desire to fly a hawk became obsessive. I searched in vain for books on the subject. I recall reading a passing description of a Cree bird trap I had come across. I reread it at least a dozen times trying to determine how to make the trap, sketching it again and again to make sense of it. I attempted to build the trap, which consisted of a bent twig, a noose, and a trigger stick, but it was never successful.

Another book detailed the capture of small birds by smearing branches with quicklime. And just where did one get quicklime? There was no quicklime store that I knew of. Maybe quicklime was available only in the tropics? And wasn't that the acid stuff that eats away flesh and bone? What would it do to my bird?

Even today books on trapping and caring for hawks are fairly rare. There are only about three thousand master falconers in the United States and Canada, along with a few hundred general and apprentice falconry license holders, some of whom seldom or never fly birds. This comprises the sum of the interest group in North America, and as a result, falconry literature is somewhat hard to find and, for the most part, esoteric, with little to offer the beginner.

At this same time I experienced the phenomenon of feeling intensely competitive with another person who also had a well-developed interest in birds. I have since observed it in bird people of all kinds, especially in bird-watchers:

> *Both potter is jealous of potter, and craftsman of craftsman; and poor man has grudge against poor man, and poet against poet.*
>
> *—Hesiod*

My competition was a boy named Steve Frewin, new to my fourth-grade classroom, and I was stung when I was displaced as the class "birdbrain" by his knowledge. His father had actually taken him hunting, and he owned a stuffed coot he claimed to have killed. I saw the tattered bird as it twisted on a wire over his bed, borax dribbling from its stitching. It had no glass eyes and its sockets were puckered shadows. The lobes of its feet were shrunken and hard, like licorice lost for a long time behind the seat of a car. It smelled bad (God bless the mothers of small, bird-crazed boys.) But he possessed this blind, black apparition and I did not.

"Shot it with my slingshot from the moving car as it flew overhead," he boasted. "Must have been a hundred feet up." Dejected, I soon deferred to Steve as he disgustingly demonstrated his considerable knowledge of birds, gained from the same *Birds of America* I owned, but seasoned with "many a trip hunting."

I regained the coveted class birdbrain title just after Christmas that year, however. A miracle happened I never could have foreseen. A family friend, while traveling, had come across the frozen carcass of a freshly killed golden eagle! Knowing my interest, he gave me the precious corpse, which I promptly lugged to school. The eagle measured more than six feet across its back from wingtip to wingtip. The gold feathers in its nape shimmered and shook whenever the carcass was moved. Most impressive were its huge feet and talons the size of bear claws.

I clearly remember, too, the matted and crusted brown feathers where a high-powered rifle slug had entered its broad chest. There would be many more golden eagles in the future, but this was the first one I was ever close to. I became more determined than ever to have a bird of prey.

With my prospects of owning a hawk dim, I had turned from hawk-hope to pigeon raising, wheedling a proper and professionally built coop from my parents as a birthday present. No sooner had the ice pigeons and long-faced, clean-legged, black-self tumblers (that's right) and Birmingham rollers begun to prosper when the fates provided me with the illusive hawk I had so long sought.

On a June morning I looked over the fence to see my teenage neighbor, Sharon, attempting to soothe a young hawk by pressing it against a bench and stroking its back. Sharon, blond, pug-nosed, broad-shouldered, slim-hipped, threw a baseball like Whitey Ford, ran the one hundred in 9.5 seconds and was a crack shot with a rifle. The young red-tail was a "brancher," meaning a young bird having recently left the nest to hop about in the branches of its tree preparatory to its first tentative flights.

As is so often the case, Sharon's boyfriend, seeking to bedazzle her, had climbed a tree and shaken the young bird to the ground, then run it down after it tired. Holding a bird tightly and stroking it with sweaty hands is a guaranteed way to sustain its panic and fear, and also removes waterproofing from delicate feathers, though I knew nothing of this at the time. As I watched with envy, Sharon carried the bird about like a football, its feet flailing and slicing her clothes and arms. Aware finally that there must be a better approach, Sharon attached a length of rope to one leg and let the red-tail hop about the lawn.

As with all youngsters who think having a hawk as a captive

looks wonderful and "cool," she was ready to throw in the towel by the end of the second day when the reality of hawk handling set in. And as with all mothers of youngsters with hawks, Sharon's mother insisted the bird be given up or taken back to its nest. This scene from my youth is reenacted every spring as kids continue to insist on taking hawks, and after they have become bored, their mothers become impatient. Without fanfare or ceremony, I became the possessor of my first hawk by default.

I called the bird Willy ("Will he really do that?"), and set about training him. I had found a copy of T. H. White's *The Goshawk* in the library (and might have found it sooner, but some soul had catalogued it under *literature*). White wrote of keeping his gos in a dark room, and whistling whenever he fed it. I blanketed the windows of my mother's laundry room and set Willy on a chair, having first bound a crude leather jess to each leg.

At first he refused to eat. But as two days passed, he became less frightened and more hungry, as all hawks eventually do, and observing that meat was offered from a human fist, he finally lunged at a fist. Unfortunately it happened to be attached to my mother's arm as she attempted to launder a batch of sheets. I was banished from the laundry room and thus deprived of further experimentation with White's techniques.

I quickly constructed a wood and chicken-wire cage and became aware for the first time of the problems created by the wire mesh: birds lunging against the biting wire cut the fleshy yellow cere along the top of their beaks and tatter their wings and tails as they turn against it in a small enclosure.

Providing food became the focus of my efforts, encouraged by my mother who was watching the family meat bill range into quadruple digits. I again called the aviary asking for advice, which was given in haste, the aviary man being busy with chores and impatient with the questions of children. He said I could feed mice, small birds, and of course, beef stew meat and chicken, now off-limits unless I was prepared to spend my own lawn-mowing money on it. My resources were better spent purchasing a few mousetraps, which I set and checked every day. My slingshot and BB gun procured English sparrows and house finches (starlings were seldom seen in the West in those days), and somehow Willy got enough to eat.

I began training Willy, having heard that getting the bird to come to the fist was the first step. Another bit of knowledge I acquired was that the falconer called his bird with the command "Ho!" In those days I could be seen wandering around with the hawk on my fist, a crude suede stocking on his head as a hood, repeating "Ho!" "Ho!" as I offered him tidbits of mice and the heads of finches.

Getting Willy prepared for flight took many weeks, but at last he was ready. (Actually it was I who had to get ready. I greatly feared losing him.) I set the bird on a perch in my backyard. After unhooding him, I walked back twenty-five feet and yelled "Ho!" Willy launched from his perch, and I watched with dismay as he promptly flew to the rooftop. The red-tail cocked his head, looking at the mouse in my hand, and trying to decide whether to come for it or depart the scene. He was just hungry enough to drop to my fist. My breath whistled out with relief; having accomplished free flight, I was not going to chance it again soon.

Any youngster is limited in patience and attention. In spite of my monomania for birds, I was no exception, and with school back in session, I soon had less than two hours of light each day in which to work the bird. Hawk training takes much time and hard work, as well as the acquisition of knowledge which has to come either from a falconry master or a good book on the art, neither of which was immediately available to a prepubescent in those days. There were also my pigeons and my peers to deal with. (I had, after all, achieved the ultimate status as a bird-child through my moment of free flight, witnessed by a friend who talked it up at school.)

Basking in the glory of having flown him once, I was encouraged by my parents to give Willy to another young aspirant. ("Can I take him whenever I want?" I asked. I was assured I could by the new would-be, which provided me the necessary rationale.) I had surprisingly little reluctance to shed myself of the hard work and dedication demanded by Willy and the art of falconry. It was my first lesson that wildlife usually make poor pets.

Willy, I am glad to say, was eventually lost to the wind by his third captor.

See-saw, the saw whet owl, reaches a full eight inches tall resting atop the chrome shade of a lamp. (Photo by Charles Trost)

3
"THE PROJECT" BEGINS

*If a tree dies, plant another
in its place.*

—LINNAEUS

Birds were seldom far from my thoughts for the next fifteen years, yet I had no time for them. First came the demands of college and a career: mother wanted me to be the governor of the state, Dad thought I should be a forest ranger, so of course I chose journalism. Then came a marriage and children which absorbed most of my time, with duck hunting and trout fishing tucked in as short respites from the hectic life of the last quarter of the twentieth century.

The rising conservation and environmental movement in the American public at large pleased and excited me, yet I could see no way to make a contribution to the gathering momentum of concern. Then, at a cocktail party one winter night, I sidled up to John Nagel, chief of the Utah Division of Wildlife Resource's (UDWR) law-enforcement section. I had gotten to know Nagel when we worked together on a television project on Utah duck hunting. A scowling, heavyset six-footer with menacing eyebrows, Nagel had an academic background in waterfowl biology. We quickly found ourselves talking birds, specifically birds of prey.

A slender, ninety-eight-pound, black-haired sprite of a woman with root-beer-colored eyes joined us. She, too, had an interest in birds that went back to her childhood in a rural Utah county. Her name was Stellanie Soter Ure, and we had been married long enough to have two sons, a Labrador retriever and a sizable mortgage on a house in the woods with a creek running by it.

"Habitat loss is the biggest single problem for *every wild thing in Utah*," Nagel expounded. "As long as Utahns continue to disregard the problems created by unlimited development, we will see less and less wildlife. And wherever raptors come in contact with humans, the raptor loses. Our conservation officers pick up a dozen birds each week—they are hit by cars, shot; they are poisoned or covered with oil . . . the list is endless," Nagel said, shaking his head.

"What happens to those birds you pick up?" asked Stel.

"We have to put 'em down, euthanize them. We can't find places for all of them in zoos and aviaries, and vets won't take them," he replied. "We don't have money or manpower to deal with them. Sometimes we take healthy, confiscated birds. We have to kill them and put them in the freezer to hold them until the trial comes up."

"In other words a human breaks a wildlife law by taking a hawk illegally, and then the hawk is confiscated, killed, and held as evidence so justice can be meted out to the human? What kind of logic is that?" I asked.

"It's the way we have to handle it," Nagel said with a shrug. "And it creates a real public-opinion problem for us," he added.

"Why couldn't citizens take these birds, hold them, care for them, nurse the sick and injured ones back to health, and release them to the wild? It would help the public-opinion problem," I said.

"It would help the *bird*," Stel snapped.

"It might be possible," Nagel said thoughtfully. "I'd have to look into it."

The next morning Stel and I stirred our first cups of coffee and watched big, wet flakes of snow plaster the trunks of cottonwood, box elder and alder trees surrounding the house. Cory, age seven, and Matt, five, padded to the table sleepily. "How would you guys like to help take care of hurt hawks?" Stel asked.

We explained as simply as we could our conversation about raptors that had carried into the wee hours, long after we were in bed and should have been sound asleep. People and their industrial artifices had created a great number of nonnatural problems for wildlife, ranging from power lines, automobiles, and glass windows into which birds flew, to chemicals, pesticides and petroleum spills. It is also human nature, we agreed, that compels some people to shoot hawks and others to take them as pets. We hoped that over time and many generations, birds of prey would develop a genetic line that could adapt to the incredible changes human beings had wrought. But for now, too many birds of prey were falling from the skies at the hands of humans.

A project to take a few hawks, help heal them, or just hold them for court disposition, would make a contribution to nature that both Stellanie and I felt we owed our world. It was something tangible we could do to be part of the solution for a world beset by industrialization, overpopulation and pollution.

Matt's pajama-covered feet swung rhythmically from the chair edge. "Why not sharks?" he asked. He was in his shark period at the time, but the discovery of gold was just around the corner.

Cory, our mechanical and musical son, was more interested in where we would keep the birds, and how. We explained the plan: build a cage in the bottoms by the creek.

"Hawks are beautiful," said Cory reflectively.

"Not as beautiful as sharks," said Matt, and the morning's first scuffle was under way.

Within a week I had called John Nagel and explained that we wanted to attempt to undertake hawk rehabilitation, that Stellanie was willing to commit time to it, and that I would help where possible.

After another week a letter granting temporary state permits arrived in Stellanie's name, directing her to work under Calvin L. Wilson, curator at Tracy Aviary. With half the necessary permits acquired, we still needed federal permission. Another period of time elapsed, and one evening I arrived from work to find a delighted Stel waving a permit from the U.S. Fish and Wildlife Service (USF&WS) allowing her to care for migratory birds, including threatened and endangered species.

Time to open shop. Stellanie called Calvin Wilson the next morning, nervously announcing we were ready to take any injured, orphaned or stray raptors. "That's nice," said Wilson gruffly. "I'll keep it in mind." Wilson was renowned for his parrot work; raptors, it was rumored, "were put head down in a bucket of water." Stel was supposed to work under this man's direction?

Stellanie contacted the USF&WS agent in Salt Lake City, where the response was more positive. He seemed pleased and interested, but very busy. He took our phone number. Next Stel called the zoo, knowing they were often asked to take wildlife picked up by citizens. They took our phone number.

We waited, assuming we were offering a needed service, unaware of the nature of public wildlife agencies which make every attempt to avoid the burden of private sector involvement. Workers in the bureaucracies had seen this before: busybody citizen volunteers who would create more work and problems for them.

"*Megalo kephali*," Stel muttered in Greek after talking with a know-it-all raptor specialist who condescended to give her five minutes of time with his views on "hawk patching" over the phone. "They know everything," she said, "so there's nothing they can learn from what I might offer."

A few of the local raptor cognoscenti shrugged and privately said that while the Ures might not do any good, they might not do any harm, either. We waited, all dressed up with no place to go.

Chong, survivor of the pair of great-horned owls, the first birds to come to the Ures. (Photo by Stellanie Ure)

4
FIRST BIRDS

The owl, night's herald

—SHAKESPEARE

The policy, it seemed, was to wait out these well-meaning, but innocent, raptor rehabilitation volunteers until they went away. Stel faithfully and regularly placed calls to the various wildlife agencies and soon she had found some friendly voices. Still, weeks passed and not a single bird turned up for us to take care of.

I was discouraged, to say nothing of being totally unprepared, when Tracy Aviary called one morning and a gruff voice said they had a pair of baby great horned owls, and would we be interested in caring for them?

Two hours later the four of us were admitted to the cool, dark interior of the green-painted, clapboard aviary building where food was prepared for distribution to the birds. An aviary worker blinked as slowly as the two downy owls that looked up at us from a box in his hands as he silently pushed it into Stel's arms.

Cory and Matt glanced curiously at the bins of peanuts, heads of lettuce, sacks of grain, and gelatinous piles of meat that were thawing on the sideboard as we passed through the building, Stel triumphantly carrying her box of great horned owl babies.

Semper paratus had been my Coast Guard operating motto, and of course my Boy Scout motto had been Be Prepared. In spite of this, I had given little serious thought to just where we would put our first charges. The boys tumbled down the hill behind the house into the bottoms, followed by Stel with the box and me with a roll of wire mesh. We took a large, saw-cut section of box-elder trunk and placed it on the moist, black earth of the shed floor; then I cut the wire to fit the shed's doorway. Stel opened the box, shook it lightly, and the two owlets shuffled into the cool darkness of the shed in the tree-shaded creek bottom.

The four of us stood back with little whispers of exclamation as the owlets focused on their new surroundings, heads swaying, huge yellow eyes dilating, great fluffy chaps of down waving softly at their flanks. The project thus began on a magic June evening when we all were smitten by two owlets with fuzzy feet and "yeepy" little voices.

Later, as Stel gingerly proffered bits of meat on long chopsticks (eliciting no interest whatsoever from the owls), we began getting to know the owlets as they evoked peals of delighted laughter. They looked comic enough—swaying, bobbing, clacking their shiny black bills and hissing if approached too closely—so we named them Cheech and Chong.

The head bobbing and swaying serves a practical purpose: it helps the owls' large eyes focus. These two youngsters, ejected for whatever reason from the comfort of their twiggy nest, were wide-eyed and fearful of us, suspiciously hissing and rising tall to defend themselves if we pressed forward, even with food, in the beginning. But they were healthy, and we had to keep them that way.

Diet became our foremost concern, with mice being first choice, but as I had learned many years before, mice were difficult to obtain. We had, however, been given a human-head-sized, frozen chunk of the carnivore feed that we had seen on the sideboards in the prep house at the aviary. When thawed, it had the consistency of chilled consommé, and while adult birds could handle it, youngsters could not scoop it up, nor would they take it from spoons. Since Stel's mentor, Calvin Wilson, had also suggested lean beef laced with cod liver oil, Stel cut up some supermarket beef stew meat and placed the oil drops on it.

She marched down to the shed and settled herself in front of the swaying, bobbing owlets. She offered the meat on a long chopstick, figuring it approximated the mother's beak and kept her far enough away from the youngsters not to alarm them. It didn't alarm them, but it didn't allure them, either. With studied indifference they glared past the meat and into Stel's eyes.

The owls might hold out forever, but Stellanie would not. Frustrated, she took a bit of meat in her fingers and held it near the beak of Cheech. The owl half closed its eyes as it reached forward and tentatively nibbled the beef, then took it from Stel's hands and gulped. The eager owlet could not have been happier than Stel was at that moment, and I watched a woman instantly transformed from hesitance to confidence, with a good measure of joy thrown in. Our owls were "started."

At the outset I was surprised at how quickly a pound of meat went down the gullets of the owl babies. We very shortly found ourselves at the supermarket in nearby Holladay village. "Cut me some really lean beef," said Stellanie to Frank, our dark-eyed, friendly butcher with the barrel chest.

"Special recipe?"

"It's for my owls," said Stel, for the first time realizing that what she was doing might be out of the ordinary. Frank winked once and took it in stride, for ours is a neighborhood of semieccentrics, including people who live with llamas and flocks of Canada geese and five-foot-long monitor lizards. There is even a lady with a hundred cats.

Stel and I conversed about raptor diet as we waited for Frank. We were now thinking ahead. "We really need mice," said Stel. Whole mice contain elements not found in lean beef, we reasoned, including the nutritional properties of the organs. And it seemed best to approximate natural foods in every way. We bought some bone meal while we waited, and then some baby vitamins.

I remembered my raptors had made pellets, or castings of hair and feathers from their prey. Was this necessary to our owls? And how would they get casting material when we were feeding strips of lean beef? We could resolve the question either by shaving Gabriel, the Labrador, or, Stel said brightly, by raiding my fly-tying kit.

Home we went with our package of owl condiments and accessories. Spreading our purchases on the kitchen counter, we set to work. I cut meat into smaller bits as Stel put a drop or two of cod liver oil on each. Then she added a pinch of bonemeal and a dropper dash of baby vitamins. A couple of rooster hackle feathers and a pinch of Lab fur, and *voilà*, owlet entrée deluxe.

Then we marched toward the shed to feed, Cory and Matt materializing like vapors from their play in the woods to watch the spectacle. The young owls gulped, eyes closed, heads back, until they had each consumed three or four ounces. At first we carried enough food to the shed to feed the owls and several adult Bengal tigers. Stel, from the beginning, insisted that each preparation be freshly made up, and that each be warmed to the approximate temperature of a fresh kill.

The search for natural food quickly led to the establishment of a small line of mousetraps around the woodpiles and near the stream. Shortly we were rewarded with our first victim, and my sons applauded as a young owl gave a final gulp and at last sat quietly, the tail of the little rodent swaying from its beak until it disappeared like a strand of spaghetti being sucked down by a fat baby.

I could have watched the growing owlets all day, and I moved a bench near the shed where we could comfortably observe the youngsters on their log perch. Owls have fascinated humans for millennia; apparently they confound the hell out of us. Some cultures say they portend death or bad luck (Sicily); others, like the Ainu of Japan, say they bring good fortune.

They are compelling creatures, on that all agree. Our owls had started life as pale white and unmarked eggs, likely laid in an abandoned hawk or magpie nest, perhaps as early as January when I have seen the Duke, as the French call him, sitting on a clutch of eggs with a cap of blizzard-driven snow between his tufts. The youngsters hatch in about thirty days, and that is when the adults prove themselves to be superb providers. When the tiny, almost-naked owlets are barely an ounce or two in weight, the adults proceed to deliver food to the nest in amounts befitting a Lucullan orgy. A typical nest may include several uneaten dead rabbits, a couple of dead ducks, a grouse, several rats, and a few snakes, all pushed to the edge of the owl-down-covered nest bowl.

Great horned owls will eat nearly anything, and I once found the feet of some domestic cats in a great-horned nest. They have killed Canada geese, coyotes, red-tailed hawks, fish, half-grown turkeys, bitterns, swans, various other owls, peregrine falcons, magpies, weasels, mink, marten, fox, and also skunks, the latter leaving a pungency that may be smelled on mounted museum owls even today, fifty years after they were collected. (Our great horneds smelled sweet, like talc, which I discovered later when I buried a nose in the fluffy breast feathers of a friendly owl.) They seem to strike at anything that moves and there are many cases of owls attempting to nab dogs and even porcupines.[1]

Owls may have some cognitive abilities; mostly they are wonderful at being *owls*. They have sight ten times better than that of humans, and offset ears on either side of the skull behind the eyes enable the owl to adeptly locate the origin of prey by sound. One of our later owls—Tufter—alerted us to the presence of birds in our area if we watched him carefully. This is lazy-person's bird watching. When he would flatten his back and turn his head to stare at the sky for long periods, we knew he was watching something overhead— often a Cooper's hawk or a falcon so high it would require binoculars for us to identify it. Some birds Tufter saw were beyond even the reach of glasses, or else he was being particularly owlish that day, for owls do seem to become fixated occasionally on certain objects invisible to us.

Owls have incredible, tined meat hooks for talons, two forward, one back, and one angling out in a deadly arrangement from which little escapes. Even those feet, however, sometimes cannot handle problem prey, as in the classic 1927 observation of a great horned that had captured a long black snake. When the owl was unable to kill it, the snake wrapped itself around the owl, constricting its wings until the observer killed the snake and freed the owl.[2]

While almost every small thing in nature seems to fear the great horned owl, few can do much about it except hide. Human beings are the owl's chief malefactors, and for years men shot the bird as a menace to poultry and game birds. Even today thoughtless gunners bring down many owls, and some are shot by biologists trying to protect peregrine falcons and other sensitive species.

Stellanie thinks it is ironical that people kill off nearly all the peregrines in the U.S. with guns and poison, but when they decide to save the peregrine, they start killing its natural enemy, alongside which it has lived in balance for forty or fifty million years. (Did I say only owls were confounding?)

There is a natural enmity between all other raptors and owls, given the voracious appetite of the owl and its insensitivity to what tastes good. Owls eat hawks and other owls, and only golden and bald eagles in turn prey on owls, possibly with no intention of eating them. I have found headless great-horned-owl remains at the foot of desert cliffs where they were most certainly captured by golden eagles during daylight roosting.

Most human intruders quickly back away from owl nesting sites. Many are the biologists and youngsters investigating owl nests who have been badly sliced by irate adult owls in hard, fast, flat-trajectory attacks at the face of the intruder. Even leather jackets are punctured and shredded, and hard hats are required equipment when one is working at owl nests. Not all nesting owls are pugs, however: one great horned reportedly used the killdeer's "broken wing" ruse to lure human intruders away from its nest.[3]

Were the two owls now with us because of human nest tampering? Or had the owl's only other predator—an eagle—left the young orphaned? We did not know, nor did anyone at the aviary. Cheech and Chong had been left, like foundlings, on the aviary steps.

One morning as I approached the shed before leaving for my downtown office, I noticed the door was ajar. Peering inside, I saw one owl swaying to and fro as she balefully glared up at me. The other was nowhere to be seen. We'd held the owls for about a week and had come to know them individually, for birds are like snowflakes: each is different in color, pattern and behavior.

I looked at the owl for a moment, realizing it was Chong. Cheech was our missing bird. A summary search around the immediate area of the shed disclosed nothing. Indifferent to my business attire,

23

I widened the search as I called Stel and the kids to come down and help look. Then I heard *clack-clack-clack*, the chopping of a young owl's beak. It seemed to come from beyond the stream. I thrashed through the underbrush and crossed the creek, and in a moment found Cheech on his belly, wings slightly spread in a kind of paralysis.

As I tried to lift him, I was neatly slashed by his long, scimitar talons, indicating that while his wings were not working properly, his feet certainly were. Carrying him into the house, Stel examined the bird as I coated my wounds with Neosporin and taped them with gauze. The boys and I watched with anxiety as Stel's fingers moved along the bird's wings, abdomen and spine. Her palpations disclosed nothing, and a call to Calvin Wilson brought only questions.

What about diet? he asked. What were we feeding? Any dogs in the area? After all, it had either been carried or had made its own way across the creek. Could it have been hit by another owl? Did we have goshawks in the neighborhood? Wilson and Stel surmised that perhaps a blow had broken Cheech's spine, causing the owl to lose the function of his wings. A cheerless Stellanie placed Cheech in the shed and decided to observe him for a few days. I went to work with a blood-flecked suit, bandaged hands, and a heavy heart.

A week passed. It had been a very hot, dry summer in the Mountain West that year. The vinca in our yard normally stood tall and crisp every day; this year its blue flowers closed and it wilted each afternoon. The woods were so dry that the neighbors were regularly checking hydrants and hoses, fearful of the repeat of a fire that had swept the cottonwoods twenty years before, doing substantial damage and terrifying everyone. Each day the sun blazed down unrelentingly.

So it was that we were altogether ready for a long-planned vacation that would take us up the cool coast of northern California, through Oregon, Washington and into British Columbia. The aviary had agreed to hold both owls for us during our vacation time. Stel had watched an unimproved Cheech long enough to realize that his damage was permanent. He would never be releasable. Stel had to make her first life-and-death decision; she waited as long as was practical, but there was no improvement. She asked the aviary to watch the bird for several days before "putting him down," the euphemism for euthanasia among animal workers.

We returned to a cooler Utah and an almost-grown Chong owl, beautifully chestnut, white and honey, with great eyelashes and feet feathered to the talons. While Stel and I knew that Cheech would not be there, the children did not, and the tears flowed. Stel puddled up as she recounted what might have been done differently to save the owlet.

For me the death of a bird is a rattling reaction of brain and gut. This recognition produces a "snick" in my brain, followed immediately by a "squish" of anguish in my stomach. The snick is the enormity of the fact that a life is gone; the squish is the flow of feeling. That flow may be melancholy at the sight of a starling lying on the grass, feathers smooth even in death from unknown causes, or it may be anger at the sight of a bird carcass blackened by oil. And worst of all, it may be guilt, which I felt to a degree in Cheech's case.

The boys were stricken. I tried to soothe them (and justify the death for myself) by explaining that in the wild, most birds died violently, that "natural causes" included being eaten, poisoned, shot or throttled. It was no consolation, and it did little to assuage my feelings of neglect at not having constructed a proper and protective pen.

Within two days of our return, we knew that a strong, constantly flapping Chong should resume her life in the wild. And why did we think Chong was a "she"? There is a consistent sexual dimorphism in raptors, with the male being approximately one-third smaller than the female. During the time Cheech had been healthy, he had been the smaller of the two owls, indicating that sexual probability, although it was no certainty, as nestling size is also dependent on hatching chronology.

Down billowed around our owl as she exercised; it was time to make our ferocious, feathered contribution to the beauty of nature's balance. On a warm July evening, Stel opened the door of the shed. We awaited breathlessly the rush of wings that would carry the owl gracefully and quietly into the deepening dusk. Chong sat on her perch blinking, digesting her "going-away" mice presented by Matt and Cory. She stared for a while, then stepped off the perch and slowly did her owl amble out the door, carefully swinging each foot out in a bobbing, shuffling walk.

Bob-bob, bob-bob. She stopped her methodical gait under a bush and preened for a few minutes. We opted to eat dinner and watch her from the patio. Without warning she took wing and landed with a fair degree of grace on a tree branch twenty-five feet above our heads. "How long could she live here?" asked Matthew, as he watched the owl while munching a barbequed hamburger. I told him of one account in which a great horned lived in captivity for twenty-nine years. When it was twenty-two years old, it was provided with a mate, which it lived with for seven years until one day it killed and ate its mate without warning.[4] "Captivity does terrible things to the best of us," I added, noting the startled look on his face.

By now Chong was a round-headed, neckless bulk silhouetted in the branches against the starlight. A car pulled into our driveway. Distracted by our visitors for a few minutes, we returned to find Chong gone. She had silently slipped into the woods.

Owl babies—in this case screech owls—were among the first birds to arrive. (Photo by Stellanie Ure)

A long-eared owl, having escaped from his box, "hides" on the headboard of a bed. (Photo by Stellanie Ure)

Tufter, a thoroughly imprinted great-horned owl, sleeps on the kitchen shelf while awaiting a phone call. He was a family favorite. (Photo by Stellanie Ure)

Four young great-horned owls in the mews. (Photo by Mike Coffeen)

*For relative size comparison, here is Pepita, a pygmy owl, on a
bathroom faucet. (Photo by Stellanie Ure)*

Matthew Ure with a downy screech owl. (Photo by Stellanie Ure)

Golden eagles on a nest. Five dangerous years to maturity. (Photo by Ray O. Kirkland)

5
HAZARDS OF THE WILD

Oh could I fly, I'd fly with thee!
We'd make swift joyful wing.
Our annual visit o'er the globe,
Companions of the spring.
—John Logan

I know of no blow more shocking to a bird-addict's ego than the realization that all his knowledge is still inadequate. Interest—even passionate interest—does not necessarily mean wisdom.

So it was that the arrival of our first two owls and the subsequent death of Cheech presented many new and unanswered questions about birds in their natural habitat and how they lived, in spite of what I thought I knew from my long acquaintance with birds of prey. Equally important for our purposes was how they met with disaster in the wild, and what we might expect to be facing as these creatures were handed along a human chain to us for help and release.

We were now acquiring a pretty good library of raptor books, and while Stellanie was curling up with medical and bird-physiology tomes, I was riffling through ornithological field literature, some of it more than a hundred years old, on the natural history of birds of prey. Books alone could not completely answer our immediate needs, and we began to spend more time observing raptors in the field. Additionally our friends with knowledge of birds were besieged with questions. One patient falconer friend finally said, "Put yourself between the wings of a bird for a while," analogous to telling us to walk in the other guy's shoes. Many biologists we knew, insistent on traditional scientific inquiry and on humanity's ability to manage wildlife, were derisive of this technique, calling it speculative anthropomorphization.

"*Bambi* was anthropomorphization," said John Nagel, "and wildlife managers are still fighting public opinion over the Disney concept that wildlife has human attributes and characteristics. It makes our job much more difficult."

Perhaps. This type of response reminds me that humanity has a need to try and control an ever-changing world, but even that, finally, is out of people's hands at the instant of the next major natural disaster. In fact fish and wildlife agencies today are practicing *human* management, and public opinion shaped by an attitude that creatures have many of the feelings and even motives of humans creates troublesome situations for wildlife biologists. I believe,though, that anthropomorphization is valuable as a means of better understanding wildlife.

Wildlife cultures and human cultures share much, both only asking for food, shelter and sex as the basics on which to build lives, and maybe not even in that order. Food and reproduction are motivators for everything that lives, and today some biologists are adapting what we have learned about human behavior as a means of evaluating wildlife behavior.

In other words raptors must have two things corresponding to human living: a bountiful kitchen and a sturdy bedroom. The kitchen is the soil-healthy hunting ground that provides flora that supports the diversity of prey utilized by the bird. It must have a certain amount of water and it must be as free as possible from chemicals and pesticides. This kitchen offers a smorgasbord table of various mice, rats, squirrels, rabbits and birds on which birds of prey can feed. Actually raptors need two kitchens: one in the area where they breed, and, equally important, a good hunting territory where they winter, especially now that so many of our western raptors migrate to Mexico and Central America where DDT and other pesticides banned in the U.S. are used extensively.

As for the bedroom, cliff faces furnish a safe haven for nesting for a variety of raptors, from eagles to falcons, while accipiters—goshawks, Cooper's hawks and sharp-shinned hawks—nest in trees. Buteos, such as red-tails, ferruginous hawks, red-shouldered hawks and broad-wings, may nest either in cliffs, on buttes, or in trees. Owls are largely tree nesters. The ideal nest cliff is protected from the hot midday sun and is difficult for humans or predators to reach. Researchers often must utilize mountain-climbing techniques to get near cliff nests, and when climbing to tree nests, they use climbing spikes.

With a good hunting territory and a good nest site, a raptor can flourish if human beings do not pressure or harass it. Most raptors are flexible and adapt to some incursion by people, but as human population grows, destruction of raptor habitat—through development, farming, draining of wetlands, and clearing of forest and rangelands—is the single largest threat to the long-term health of raptor populations. You can save all the bedrooms—the nesting areas—but if birds don't have a kitchen, they can't survive.

Given reasonably high-quality hunting and breeding areas, how do you begin to understand the bird in its natural setting? I opted to take traditional science, then pretend I was a bird, applying the data I had learned as it seemed appropriate. By this method I began piecing together how birds lived in the wild, what rigors they faced, and what they needed for survival.

Imagine, if you will, being a bird—a golden eagle, just beginning life in a nest on a butte near the Hoback River in western Wyoming. Your eyes, three days after birth, are beginning to open, and you can discern that you are on a cliff face looking northeast across a gently rolling landscape of lavender sage, transected by woolly bursts of reddening willows in the creek bottoms. On the slopes that grade upward to the south, stands of aspen are misted with lime hues as the sun urges them into spring. Surrounding them are the undulating stairways of pine that climb into the snowfields still clinging to the peaks.

You are cloaked in gray down that compliments your gray-colored feet and beak. For a few moments you can hold your head up, but it droops slowly to rest on the fresh pine boughs that always line the nests of golden eagles in the West. Supporting the fragrant greenery of the nest's top layer is a towering pillar of sage, aspen and pine branches, built up over two hundred years by a score of generations of golden eagles. Below, in the entwined limbs, a pair of sage sparrows make their home with impunity.

A shadow falls over the nest as mother eagle arrives from a brief flight that has resulted in the capture of a kangaroo rat, which she promptly and efficiently skins with her beak. You are offered selected slivers, which you gobble blindly and randomly until your crop bulges like the breasts of a fat matron. Dinner served, mother spreads the bare brood patch on her breast and shuffles gently over you, her feathers fluffed to capture and enfold you. Huge, powerful talons are harmlessly knuckled inward as she settles over you, enveloping you in down-soft, radiant warmth, protection against the chill of the coming night and the growing wind. Mother closes her "third eyelid"—the nictitating membrane—against the sleet of winter's last hurrah, and lies flat in the nest cup, her feathers overlapping with the sticks and boughs.

At the age of ten days, if you had a mirror, you would notice that your eyes are deep black-brown and bulgy, and that the gray hairlike down of hatching is being replaced by handsome white wool. At twenty days you proudly note the glossy black feathers that are bursting through at your wingtips, tail and rump like a chocolate cake bursting through its layer of white frosting.

By now your youthful curiosity wants to learn something about eagle family history. There is a place on the north slope of the Wind River Mountains called Willow Lake. Since your mother was hatched there ten years ago, you call her Willow. Your father, hatched seven years ago on a shale butte not far from the flyspeck town of Daniel, is known as Daniel.

You may think that it is because your mother is older that she is larger, a common misconception shared by humans (who often think crows are baby ravens, and Brewer's blackbirds are baby, baby ravens). The female Willow is larger than the male Daniel by a third as in all birds of prey, a fact not lost on medieval falconers who called the male bird a "tiercel" for this reason. The nest in which you live was used three seasons ago, part of an alternating group of nests probably passed in a genetic line through many generations of your predecessors.

The Hoback nest site of the family was homesteaded two hundred years ago by Canny Eagle and Wary Eagle, who sought respite from the constant demand for eagle feathers by Crow Indians in their old territory in the Absaroka Mountains. But the site had other important qualifications: it boasted three kinds of sage and rich grasses that supported white-tailed and black-tailed jackrabbits, Uintah ground squirrels, abundant numbers of sage grouse, several species of mice and rats, antelope, bison, deer and elk, all of which provided a variety of food, including carrion in spring from the big game. There was fresh water in creeks that flowed from the slopes of the Wind Rivers, and fresh pine for nest material.

Until a hundred years ago, the land was pretty much unchanged. The white man's arrival brought cattle and sheep, decimating the herds of big game (extirpating the bison). But you eagles are very *adaptable*, and you quickly learned that dead cattle and sheep can be fed upon, and that occasionally it is possible to capture a fresh-born lamb, for which some of you have acquired an unhealthy taste that has given all golden eagles a bad reputation in the West.

At age forty-five days, you're the equivalent of a sublimely confident ten-year-old kid. At five-and-a-half pounds, you can now stand on one leg and doze, and it bothers you hardly at all that Mom and Dad are gone for long periods. You are big enough now to handle your own defense against the only possible predator (other than human beings) that a baby eagle has: a demented great horned owl with an empty stomach. You've learned to scratch and preen with vigor, and when you do, you notice that great billows of down break from your blood-filled feather shafts as more and more feathers replace your wool. Oh yes: you are learning to flap your awkward wings.

You strut and preen, pouncing unmercifully on unwary sticks or an old rabbit leg, the latter contributing to the nuisance of a thousand dermestid beetles which scour the nest, cleaning the rotting overabundance of food left by your parents, and getting in your eyes, nostrils and ears.

Now you are sixty-five days of age, sophisticated, worldly, flapping dexterously at the nest edge as you look out across the rolling sage below. A rock squirrel has climbed way out on the end of an elderberry branch. Why, he'd be a cinch to catch, if you could only fly. And you are always *hungry*. Where's the Old Lady with dinner, anyway? (Yes, you are now the equivalent of a teenaged human.) *Chuk! Chuk! Chuk!* You call loudly. The name sticks.

You are perched on the edge of the nest when the first crack of a rifle thunders up the butte and sends a shower of nest splinters into your cheeks and breast. A shiny truck parked far below has meant nothing; you have seen distant humans before. But there is malice in the sound as men with rifles continue firing at the nest; you flatten yourself against the rock behind the nest. An eternity later, the thunderous noise ceases, the humans drive away. Humbling, and a learning experience even for a cocky teenager, as Great-grandmother Wary's gene finds its proper place in the development of your character.

Life in the nest has been relatively sheltered. Since you are an "only eagle," you have never known the Cain and Abel syndrome, in which the larger (usually the first-hatched) eaglet kills its smaller brother or sister by taking its food and gradually pecking it to death. Food has been abundant this spring, and only the single incident with human gunners mars the serenity of your nestling days.

Time to face the real world. Your first flight is from the nest to a grassy hillside a hundred yards away, and since you know little about dropping your flaps for a soft landing, you tumble beak over teakettle and arise from your cloud of dust panting and alarmed, but exhilarated. You soon become more adept, thanks to the urging of your mother, who sweeps by carrying food, forcing you to follow and master the air currents if you wish to eat. Your flights are sloppy and slow, but within days you are able to soar high over the prairie with Daniel and Willow.

Your first attempts at killing food are little more than controlled crashes, any one of which might break a wing or neck, thus checking you out of the game of life at a tender age, as happens to many eaglets. In each case the prey escapes.

One August morning you dive on a black-tailed jackrabbit and surprisingly, your zig matches his zag and suddenly you have a tentative grip on him. A big jackrabbit in a loose clutch is like trying to hold a berserk windmill, and those powerful hind legs paddle you like trip hammers. You haven't yet learned that a sharp nip to the base of the skull will dispatch him, so you clumsily start to eat him as he writhes and thumps, until at last he bleeds to death and, shaken and ruffled, you stand atop him, screaming in victory.

September: the butter yellow aspen sing like tenors in counterpoint to the dark green basso of the pines and firs. A cold wind boils in from the north, and Willow and Daniel set their wings and mount higher as slate clouds flick their tongues southward, spitting the first pellets of snow. This way, this way, they signal, and you join a host of other birds—ospreys, sharp-shinned hawks, red-winged blackbirds and cinnamon teal, all fluttering like autumn leaves before the front.

It is easiest to set your wings and tail and catch the wind as it hurls you south along the face of a mountain range. In less than an hour, you are sixty miles from the Hoback. Daniel and Willow are nowhere to be seen, and you call out in panic. Some young eagles may spend a year, even more, with their parents. But now you are an orphan of the storm, on your own in a hostile, hungry world.

You try to beat back into the wind, calling for your parents. A great kettle of Swainson's hawks boils by on the first leg of an eight-thousand-mile flight to Argentina. A gregarious group of young red-tails whips past doing aerobatics, like teens on an outing. You are exhausted fighting the blow. The wind relentlessly pushes you into the Wasatch Mountains, and at dusk you alight in a huge, dead pine on a ridge on Willard Peak. As night falls, you see a thousand lights like a carpet of stars along the broad valley on the edge of Great Salt Lake.

At first light you are off again, and in the distance you are heartened to see a golden eagle as it skims the snow-dusted peaks. You sideslip down to the bird, but it quickly mounts toward you hostilely, head up, prepared for battle, unsure of your intentions. Mounting higher, you drift with the wind hour after hour.

Almost imperceptibly, it becomes warmer. The tans, grays and browns of the earth have taken on new and fanciful colors and shapes. This is juniper and red-rock country, a jumble of deep canyons, blocky buttes, and wind- and water-cut rincons—amphitheaters scoured in the layer cake of sediments set down by ancient lakes and oceans. As darkness falls, you pull up under a ledge in a Wingate sandstone cliff, oblivious to the black square of window cut into a nearby Anasazi dwelling seven hundred years before. It is a place only an eagle can see. That night the winter storm lays down its full force. In the morning the red rocks stand in bloodlike contrast to the white mantle of snow. You have come nearly four hundred miles.

As you ride the thermals rising from the steaming cliff face in the morning sun, you are joined by another young golden eagle, then a third. Birds of the year congregate to learn two flight techniques, attack and evasion, and like wrestling youngsters are soon mounting high, then diving and sideslipping in short, swirling attacks. A dozen ravens spy your play and soon join you in a column that rises two thousand feet; the ravens attack, then fall away on soft, liquid strokes as you dive on them, never quite getting them within talon reach.

With your new-found eagle friends—called Durango and Vernal for their places of origin—you find perches within a few hundred yards of one another and preen and rouse, shaking loose feathers from your plumage, mending separated barbels. Perhaps a cock of the head or a short chirp is the signal for the three of you to launch on the afternoon thermals, and after an hour of drifting, you come to a valley surrounded by red-rock cliffs. A river meanders through the valley, and geometric fields attach themselves to its coils.

Ducks! A flight of teal bursts from the water and you dive, targeting the forward bird, but are thwarted as the bird twists away. The trailing bird, however, chooses to climb, and then banks in an attempt to drop into the safety of the willows. In an instant your long leg shoots forward and grips the duck across the back.

You settle onto a dead cottonwood to enjoy your meal, where you are set upon by Vernal, who has been slow in his hunting, and would rather chase you for his dinner. Durango, meanwhile, sits with a crop full of a cottontail rabbit he captured as it ran from its willow-side burrow in the river bottom. You are prepared to fight Vernal, and you mantle your duck, lifting your wings around it as you scream with menace. Vernal stays close, hoping for scraps, but there are none, as the teal is small and you are very hungry.

You learn to feed on a variety of prey—dropping time after time from a fence post onto a colony of small *microtus* mice—until you can eat no more. One evening you find a brown trout washed up on a sandbar in the river, and you eat it, too.

As the days pass, Vernal has little success at hunting; you notice that he seems to move slowly, hesitantly, and more and more often tries to beg scraps from your kills. Vernal grows weaker, and one morning after a storm, he lies beneath his cottonwood perch on the red earth, his head extended and his eyes closed. By the end of the day, he is dead. Durango dies differently a few days later, zapped by thousands of volts of electricity from a wire line that soars and falls on poles that march across the distant buttes.

Other young eagles fledged that year drift into the territory during the winter. Two of them have learned to live off road kills, and they are fat. One is killed by a truck on a two-lane asphalt highway twenty miles north of the river, and the other dies an agonizing death from a sheep carcass poisoned for coyotes. Yet another eagle is caught in a leg trap, also set for coyotes, and twists its leg off to gain freedom, only to die of infection. A young eagle from the San Rafael Swell is struck in the breast by a high-powered slug from the rifle of a bored deer hunter.

Of all the young eagles that drifted into the valley that winter, you alone survive to drift north to the Hoback in the spring. If you are smart and lucky, you may make it to breeding age—five years.

These are some of the perils faced by a raptor in just its first and most vulnerable year, the period when biologists agree that about 80 percent of all youngsters die or are killed. Young birds are sloppy fliers and, like young humans, seem to feel invincible, and this may contribute to their death rate.

Certain species have specialized problems: ground-nesting harriers, for instance, whose eggs or young may be crushed by early hay mowings in farmlands. Burrowing-owl habitat in much of the West is going quickly, replaced by industrial parks, malls and subdivisions; burrowers are also poisoned through prairie-dog eradication programs. Short-eared owls nest and hunt in ever-declining wetlands, and ferruginous hawks are particularly sensitive to any nearby disturbance while brooding their eggs, and will abandon their nests.

I suspect that many raptors have become more wary of human beings—their "unwary gene" having been snuffed in the great raptor kill-offs of the nineteenth and early-twentieth centuries. Yet as the human population continues to grow, people keep throwing wildlife curves, such as the automobile, nonspecific predator poisons, construction projects and power lines.

That was why we were in business.

Circus the marsh hawk, or northern harrier, an instant before he left the box for Cory's back, then to freedom. (Photo by Jim Ure)

6
Mews Musings

He who hurts the little wren
Shall never be beloved by men
—Blake

Knowing what raptors were experiencing in the wild was vital to help us in improving diagnosis of illness and injury, preparing proper diet and understanding normal bird-of-prey behavior, but at a very basic and practical level, the next important challenge we faced was in providing proper caging in our own backyard.

After our initial, lengthy wait for Cheech and Chong, little did we expect our next birds to come so quickly, and we had taken a respite from thinking about our next steps. Within a week of Chong's parting flight, Tracy Aviary called with two more birds, an immature northern harrier, or marsh hawk, and a kestrel, or sparrow hawk, both left at the aviary in apparent good health by persons unknown under circumstances unexplainable—a bird in a box on the porch, like a foundling. Could we get them the next day?

Thinking noble thoughts but remiss in noble deeds, I had to start crash construction of a hastily considered cage, a first mews, or hawk barn. Cory and I set about the project that evening, marking off an area along the creekbed where we could construct a suitable cage (after first moving Matthew and his gold-panning operation downstream a rod or two. Matthew was absolutely fixated on finding gold in our tributary to Big Cottonwood Creek, and spent hours gently swishing his pan in the bone-chilling waters of the snow-fed stream).

Selecting a spot beneath a huge, narrow-leafed cottonwood, surrounded on three sides by alder and box elder, we marked off a ten-by-ten-foot space, well exposed to the south sun because I recalled that my own birds had enjoyed soaking up sun on winter mornings and after bathing. It also provided shelter from the northwesterly storms that predominate in our area of the Great Basin, as well as shade from the summer sun, although our woods

41

were at least ten degrees cooler than the rest of the valley, thanks to the stream and canyon breezes.

We clattered off in the station wagon on an expedition to the local hardware store and returned with the necessary lumber, nails, and a roll of one-inch-mesh chicken wire. By the end of the next afternoon, we stood back to look at the nearly finished product. Hardly a work of art, but it was serviceable: six feet tall, with a solid wall on the north, a sturdy frame covered by wire mesh, and a door made of two ten-inch-wide planks joined by a rudimentary Z nailed across them. We placed a couple of cut logs inside for perches, commandeered (at great personal sacrifice) one of Matt's gold pans for water, and departed to pick up the birds from the aviary.

"The big hawk will eat the little one," said Cory presciently, as the assistant curator put the birds in boxes.

"Not if you keep the big hawk well fed," admonished the curator, waving good-bye as we drove home with our two birds.

We placed them in the new enclosure, where the little kestrel immediately began preening his bluish secondary feathers, rousing himself with vigor. He was in good health. The harrier, looking ancient and wild-eyed, flew directly into the chicken-wire mesh and suddenly, sinkingly, I recalled what a poor cage covering it made, especially for birds which throw themselves to "bate" against the wire. I could already see the skin on his nares—the fleshy yellow tissue at the base of the beak in which the nostrils are located—beginning to bleed slightly from a wire cut. He would survive with only superficial cuts I knew, but I muttered darkly at my bad memory and lack of foresight about the chicken wire as we walked up the hill toward the house and dinner.

In just minutes we heard the sharp *kee-kee-kee-kee* of the terrified kestrel, caught fast in the talons of the harrier, about to become a meal. Four of us galloped down the hill and bounded into the cage. I wrested the little bird from the grip of the larger harrier, getting my hands sliced by the talons of both birds as they gripped me in their own separately motivated terror: little hawk of big hawk, big hawk of me.

What now? The kestrel, dubbed Star by Matthew after he had heard the bird's scientific name, *Falco sparverius*, was temporarily placed in a cardboard box as the boys raced off to borrow a wire bird cage volunteered by a helpful neighbor. The harrier, wild-eyed, beak open, sat back on his tail, wings wide, breathing rapidly, no doubt wondering what the next round of combat would bring. Stel put a chicken leg in with the panting bird, but he ignored it in our presence.

The neighbor's cage proved very temporary indeed, for two

days later our Labrador retriever, Gabriel, broke into the cage and left it birdless and overturned. He was, after all, a bird dog, Stel opined, torn between loyalty to our longtime family duck dog and the newly acquired kestrel. For the first time we began to see the problems of keeping dogs and birds together. We had been accustomed to letting Gabriel out of his kennel to run before his meals. Additionally a jealous Gabriel had now taken to peeing on Stel's feet whenever she came to visit with him in his kennel, his ego and intelligence offended by Stel redirecting her attentions to these feathered creatures that were now a part of the household activity.

We assumed Star had escaped when the dog turned over the cage, but a few days later, as I worked clearing weeds in the vinca that was growing like a lush carpet beneath the trees off the west side of the house, I found the kestrel's carcass, feet drawn up, wings carefully folded. I did not think he had been killed outright by the dog, for he was trained to carry things quite gently. (A couple of years before, he had come home with a dozen of the neighbor's eggs carried carefully in his mouth, having snagged them off a porch just after the arrival of the milkman. He had also retrieved a string of Christmas tree lights and a ski boot in the course of his neighborhood roamings.)

I never did tell the children I had found Star dead; four birds received, two birds dead this early in the rehabilitation game seemed ominous, and though it was foolish to think I could protect the kids from the emotions of living with wild things, it seemed appropriate at the moment. They had been so affected by Cheech's death.

A friend had long desired this well-trained gun dog, so with some reluctance, I sent him to the fellow at his farm near the duck club, where I am happy to report he lived a long, happy life.

Circus was our only bird and getting stronger every day; he had come to us without injury, but by feeling the bird's keel, or breastbone, an old pigeoner's technique, one could quickly tell what kind of condition the bird was in. Circus had a sharp keel, with little muscle tissue on either side, a sign that he probably had not had much to eat for some time before we got him, and was using this supply of fat and muscle to survive on. There were also "hunger traces" in the feathers of his tail—weaknesses which result when young birds or birds in moult do not have proper nutrition or are under stress, analogous, some say, to the stress marks we humans may see in our own fingernails due to dietary or traumatic changes. We were fearful that Circus would break his tail, as he banged into the caging whenever we approached. After fattening him for a couple of weeks, we felt it was time to release him.

The job fell to Cory and I and, cameras in hand, we drove the twenty-eight miles to the Farmington Bay Waterfowl Refuge, reasoning that he was, after all, a marsh hawk before he had been renamed by the American Ornithological Union. Actually we have seen harriers virtually in every kind of ecosystem here in the West—mountain summits, sagebrush flats, and farmlands.

We parked the car and with Circus in a cardboard box, we walked a short distance down the Turpin Dike road. I set the box on the ground and Cory positioned himself in front of it to get a photo of Circus leaving. I opened the box and Circus immediately jumped on Cory's back, where he paused for an instant as if to gather his wits, then leaped to a nearby dirt pile, perhaps to establish a sense of wind direction. We turned to focus our cameras and to allow for the thundercloud-broken light filling the sky over Great Salt Lake on this lovely summer afternoon. The harrier spread his wings and pushed off the mound, caught the wind, and sailed south over the marshland in firm, strong strokes, growing smaller and smaller against the billowing cumulus clouds.

The hair on my neck and head tingled with elation as the bird disappeared. Damn! That's what this is *all* about, I thought, savoring a feeling of deep satisfaction.

Cory and I rewarded ourselves with a burrito from our favorite Mexican restaurant on the way home, to cries of "unfair" from Stel who was sitting with Matthew, now recovering from a tonsillectomy. She was given a detailed description of the release, and this was more satisfying than any meal, she said pluckily, in part for Matt's benefit, as he was a burrito afficionado and by now sick of Jell-o.

A male kestrel was the next bird in our cage, and when we received an immature red-tail the next day, we realized that the departure of the dog had given us a bonus: we now had his big chain link kennel as a bird holder. With a roof of wire and perches placed inside, it would serve to hold any larger hawks that we might receive. Stel remarked that the creek bottom near the house was starting the look like a Joad family encampment, with makeshift wire cages, tarpaulins, tipped-over buckets, an old picnic table and the original metal shed.

Autumn was upon us before we knew it, and birds came and went, including a one-eyed owl we called, naturally, Cyclops. Stel released the bird with some reluctance, wary of what its future in the wild might be, to be comforted later by the knowledge that many one-eyed and one-legged birds have been found healthy and breeding in the wild.

Winter retreated before the onslaught of crocuses and Bohemian waxwings moving north; now we could smell the earth again. As the buds swelled, so did our bird load. They came uncertainly at first, from a couple referred by the aviary, from a shy UDWR conservation officer, and eventually from a USF&WS agent, a cautious, unspoken indication that we had either been accepted, or at least deemed a practical receptacle for problems that were otherwise difficult to dispose of.

In ones and twos we received them: broken birds that had to be euthanized, dinged birds with drooping wings, birds missing tail feathers, birds with clipped beaks, birds with painted toenails, birds that quickly filled our available space and presented us once again with demands for caging. What we needed, Stel and I decided, was a real mews, built to falconer's specifications, with high ceilings and slatted openings on the front and top, made entirely of wood and preferably with an escape-prevention entry chamber, like two doors with a safety lock. It was going to be expensive to build such a structure, and for the moment seemed far out of reach.

Necessity being the mother of invention, we turned to a time-honored method of temporarily securing birds: the falconer's perch, used to "weather" and stake birds, usually while they were awaiting either training or hunting flights. The use of this perch was necessitated by the arrival of a female red-tail, Artemis, when every cage space we had was full. This bird was especially troubling to Stellanie, as Artemis came to us in a sorry state. Her cere was cut from banging against raw cage wire, her feet were cracked and torn, her primaries and tail feathers were in tatters, and she was very skinny, as Stel's palpations quickly revealed.

We knew little of her history with humans (as usual), and my guess was that she had been found with a broken wing, probably gunshot by spring rabbit hunters, then contained in a small cage for many weeks until she was given up to the aviary, which turned her over to us. The wing had healed badly and hung down at an odd angle. She was a difficult case because this was a bird with no future but death. She could neither be placed with a falconer, nor given to a zoo for display, nor could she be released. Even with us, she was taking space and resources that might be dedicated to a bird with a better chance at being returned to the wild. Were we in business to provide a haven for all birds forever, regardless of their prognosis?

We were in business to rehabilitate and release as many birds as possible. But I had not foreseen until now the difficulty of the philosophical questions that might be outgrowths of that operating ethic. Not wanting to face the first euthanization situation immediately, we turned to the block perch for temporary respite, hoping perhaps that a school class or citizen might somehow show up to take the bird.

Following patterns provided by falconers, I drove a forty-inch length of concrete reinforcing rod into a ten-inch-long section of cottonwood branch approximately eight inches across. By pounding the rod in with a hammer, I insured it fit snugly and could not be pulled off. Next Stel "cast" Artemis in a towel, which means she wrapped her loosely in mummylike fashion to immobilize the bird's wings and feet. The feet of a bird of prey are its weapons, so we seldom needed to fear a beak, although Stel was once nipped smartly on the lip by a bald eagle, and sharp, needle-point kestrel bites were too numerous to mention.

Leather jesses, like slender bracelets, were then placed around the ankles of the bird, and were secured to a five-foot-long leather leash by means of a Sampo deep-sea fishing swivel. Finally a three-inch-diameter ring (we used horse tack—a harness ring) was slid over the reinforcing rod, the rod and block were driven into the earth, and the leash was tied to the ring around the rod by means of a falconer's knot, which secures it tightly but allows for relative ease of release, even when the leather is wet.

This perch provides the bird with a fairly large, flat space on which to sit, and the swivel allows it to move around the perch. The bird may fly down to the ground for the distance allowed by the leash. It may also bate against the leash and firmly planted block for exercise. A carefully built block perch will not damage the bird's tail or wing feathers. Block perches can pose a danger to birds, for they can get tangled up, and a dangling bird left in the sun can quickly expire, so birds on block perches must be checked on regularly. My particular log-and-rod perches were quite crude, but Artemis now had a comfortable, secure perch without wire or bars.

By late May the mock orange was exploding with blossoms, and it seemed as if clutches of baby kestrels and injured adult kestrels would not stop coming. They were confiscated from children who had robbed nests, rescued from wind-downed trees, saved from the wrecker's ball in old buildings, and found in farm fields, unable to fly, victims of cars. Our cage space was completely filled by larger birds. First I tried building some small block perches for these kestrels, the tiniest and most exquisite of North American falcons, but these miniblocks were not satisfactory, as tail damage seemed to be inevitable.

We turned next to the bow perch, usually used by falconers for accipiters. This perch is a steel-rod bow mounted on a circular base of quarter-inch plate steel, which provides ample weight to keep the perch from tipping. I found a willing welder who, for ten dollars each, cut me the base disc and shaped the rod in an arc, after first putting on one of our harness rings. I padded the bow with soft cloth, wrapped it in twine, then covered this padding with leather, sewing it with a regular needle and waxed thread. We jessed, swiveled and leashed a kestrel, just as before, and attached the leash to the ring. Then we watched carefully as our first kestrel preened, bated and test-drove the prototype for us without incident. The small bow even proved reliable on the seat of a car, its weighty base firmly anchoring it. This perch proved to be ideal for all smaller hawks, but heavy enough to cause a hernia when one had to lift a perch like this made for larger birds.

You really can't jess and perch baby birds, and when they came in clutches of five or six of the little fellows, downy heads tilted back as they chirred for food, we were forced to look at yet another container—the humble cardboard box. Millennia ago falconers learned that a hood will keep a bird sitting quietly, and the cardboard box became for us that calming hood. Its modifications were simple: a large box closed at both ends, with small light slits cut out. Into this container we poured our first clutch of downy kestrels. They huddled in the corner fearfully as we lifted the lid to offer bits of chicken during the first twenty-four hours they were with us. By the beginning of the second day, they were already announcing their eagerness with a hungry chirr at the first touch of the box. Eventually opening the box created a minor peril, as young kestrels would make attempts to clamber out. Their wing fanning threw great billows of powdery down into the air, and first one, then another, would hop to the edge of the box to have a look at the outside world. Oddly we also observed a rapid foot movement, like a dance, among the young kestrels in anticipation of feeding. Cory named this the "sparrow hawk shuffle."

The box was also ideal for treating birds recovering from a variety of ailments, including trauma. A cardboard box is not only dark, but its sides are smooth and difficult for even a large bird to tear open (I was later surprised, however, at how much cardboard box small owls can chew, although we never experienced this phenomenon with other birds). Additionally the box sides give way when a bird presses against them, and this softens any attempts the bird may make at trying to get out. When in a properly sized box, a bird cannot get up the momentum to harm itself by flying against its sides. Our birds kept this way were calm and quiet in the semidarkness. At first we cut the light slits at the top of the box, and found the occupants would jump up when they saw us on the way to them with their food. Sometimes a taloned foot would shoot out as I walked past a box, as if flagging me for attention. Since birds in captivity are quickly conditioned to the food stimulus created by the appearance of a keeper, we moved the slits to the bottom of the box, which kept the birds calmer, especially important for a bird with a healing wing or a shattered foot.

When startled, even a bird in pain will jump and attempt to fly against the side of the box, so, of course, we moved the boxes to the quiet part of the house—the master bedroom. Soon a half-dozen boxes placed around the bedroom were not uncommon, and I had to snake and weave past taloned feet reaching out from box bottoms for my hairy, pink, mouselike toes as I trotted to and from the shower.

We always spread fresh newspaper in the bottom of the box but noticed early on that larger birds especially would foul their tails when they muted in the box bottom, a problem easily rectified by placing a rock or sturdy log on the bottom of the box as a perch. Soon we placed sticks in boxes where babies were kept, and under the boxes of youngsters we always kept a heating pad turned to a low setting. Stel also insisted a heating pad be put under any bird that had undergone surgery or was in shock.

Stel made another decision: we would not reuse any box since it could cause contagion. So began an endless search for boxes, which up to this time had been a colorful variety of containers marked "Benny's Apples," "Hack Chemicals," "Head Man Brand California Cool Cucumbers" and "Pampers." As a means of shorthand, we had decided to call each bird by the name of its box, and as a result we soon had an owl named Benny Apple, and a kestrel called Cool.

I reasoned there must be a source for boxes wholesale and in standard sizes, because I was becoming a notorious dumpster diver in our neighborhood, and some people we knew had seen me standing at the back door of the liquor store as if awaiting a handout. "JUST GETTING BOXES FOR HAWKS, heh, heh, heh," I waved to my passing friends and smiled wanly.

The box dilemma was solved after I found a company in the Yellow Pages that made and distributed boxes by the jillion. I needed ten to twenty at a time, not two thousand, but a voice on the phone seemed to indicate they could fill my order.

I found the Box Place in a dank, dilapidated part of town beneath a notorious viaduct, not a stone's throw from the old Union Pacific and Denver and Rio Grande Western railroad depots, long-ago transportation centers in a once-healthy part of a downtown that had grown, swarmed around the depots, and moved on, leaving only dusty windows, derelicts, and a few industrial-supply places.

There was another problem: the owner of the Box Place was both deaf and drunk much of the time. "How do you do?" I said to the back of the owner's head as he watched a flickering black-and-white television set in the cluttered, dark office, while a sooty-looking, ring-necked pheasant gazed down at me with glass eyes from its roost on a paper-covered filing cabinet. On a threadbare, ancient, clipped, blue-velvet sofa pushed against the wall sat a gold-fringed, white-satin pillow with "USMC, Yokosuka" emblazoned over a map of Japan.

The man whistled as he sat in his chair, and suddenly whirled on me. "What's that?" he replied, pulling a large, pearl-handled pistol from his drawer. The look in his eye was not unlike that of the wild, suspicious harrier we had placed in our cage the previous summer.

Taken aback, I repeated: "How do you do?" It sounded very tentative to me, too.

"Ohhh," he said, dropping the revolver with a clatter into the drawer. "I thought you said 'Hang it in your ear.'" He sagged back into his chair. "Sometimes I get so mad. You can't be too careful these days. Cops won't help you. I had a guy try to hold me up with a knife. I pulled out my pistol and chased him out into the alley. My first shot missed and hit the radiator of an Audi. Second shot hit the guy in the butt. Blood and antifreeze all over the sidewalk. Didn't hurt the guy much; he was in the hospital for a few days 's all. He's on trial; I'm on trial. Cops won't help you."

He seemed as sincere as a deaf drunk could be, and I sympathized, for I had lost about 10 percent of my hearing as a result of some errant, too-close shots made by hunting friends from the same duck blind, and through the use of a power saw while I was clearing brush at home. In those days I had never thought to protect my ears.

After several repeats, and several "whats?" from each of us, he took my order and disappeared into the gloomy interior of his warehouse, where I could see flattened boxes stacked to the ceiling.

He returned a few minutes later. "What did you say you were going to put in these boxes?"

"Hawks," I said loudly.

He looked at me for a long time. "Oh. I thought you said dogs. Does it matter if the boxes got writing on 'em? I have a bunch of rejected commercial boxes I can give you real cheap . . . forty cents each."

"They'll be fine," I said.

The man disappeared again into the gloom, where the deep booms of a dog bark emanated. He attempted to return a minute later. Even when flat, large boxes take a lot of room. He was carrying them with arms spread wide—too wide for the entry door—and sent himself sprawling and cursing against a nearby fire extinguisher, which fell to the concrete floor with a bang and immediately began discharging a raging fog into the warehouse and tiny office, its roar punctuated by the dog barks. "Let's just go outside," he said, pulling a pint from his desk drawer. We sat on the stoop, occasionally looking back inside to see if the fog was thinning.

With pint half in hand and half in belly, he seemed a different, more amiable man, none the worse for his tumble. "Y'know, there's bald eagles in Utah."

"Yes. Lots of them come down in winter from Canada and Alaska," I replied.

"Summer, too."

"Some are what?"

"IN SUMMER, TOO," he said, cupping his hand around his mouth.

"Oh. I've never see them in summer," I said. There were no nesting bald eagles in Utah, according to the UDWR.

"I seen white-headed eagles in June."

"Where?"

"I dunno. I have to ask my kid. He showed 'em to me."

"Yes. Do that," I said, dismissing the observation impatiently. "Can we get the boxes now?"

"I guess we can breathe in there," he said, looking back into the hazy office.

Inside, everything was covered with thick, white dust from the extinguisher. I picked up the boxes, paid Mr. Box, and he laboriously wrote me a receipt, an act which took nearly as long as the time it had taken to find the boxes and bring them out. "Come back soon," he said, wiping a path on his desk with his fist, " 'n' I'll check on those eagles for you."

"Do that," I said. And I thanked him. As I left, I mused on my own hearing problems, and how news reports had recently led me to believe that "a thousand Turds fled Iraq for the border of Turkey," and a commercial had encouraged me to buy "chili-flavored Rolaids" (they were cherry flavored, I learned, much to my everlasting disappointment).

Yippee. A steady source of boxes for birds in need of dark and quiet so they might heal without harming themselves. Boxes, oodles of boxes; clean, one-owner boxes without wrinkles or loose tops. The box provides easy access to the patients, for you can reach in through the collapsible corners of the folded-in top and leave very little room through which a bird can escape. We did have a few birds get out, usually from wrinkled boxes obtained from a local store. If the top of the box is too loose and floppy due to prior use, a bird may force its head and shoulders into the opening and eventually escape. It was startling to walk into the bedroom and be greeted by the expectant chirp of a red-tailed hawk, or to find an owl perched on your bed or chair. This happened only once or twice, and fortunately, because the bedroom door was always kept shut, none of the other birds on perches in the house were harmed.

One day a radio commercial puzzled me: a hotel was offering ballet service. It took a moment for the realization to dawn that it was my hearing again, and this reminded me that I must return to the Box Place, for we were running low.

"I need some more boxes in assorted sizes," I told Mr. Box, explaining that kestrels needed little boxes, owls and red-tails needed medium boxes, and eagles needed big boxes. I was prepared for nearly anything when I visited his warehouse this day.

"Walk this way," he said, so I did. We passed through a door and I was immediately set upon by the Doberman behind the bark I had heard on my previous visit. "Oh, I forgot about the dog," he said, as I struggled to free myself from its death grip on my sleeve.

"Quite a surprise," I said, fitting my torn coat together to see if it could be mended.

"Oh, this is my son," he said, pointing to a young, bearded man on the telephone. He was sitting inside an inner office, a small, barewood room in the bowels of the warehouse.

"You're the guy with the eagles," this young man said amiably as he hung up the phone and his father shuffled off in search of boxes for me. "Yep. I've seen white-headed eagles the last two, three years when I've floated the Westwater."

"What time of year?" I asked, always the birder's second question.

"May and June," he said.

"You're sure?"

"Positive. These are bald eagles."

We talked a while. The son was savvy about wildlife, and I believed he was indeed seeing bald eagles on the Westwater, a tributary to the Colorado River in eastern Utah. I told him if they were there at that time of year, they almost had to be nesting. This was a first as far as I knew. I got a more specific location from him.

"Here's your boxes," said his father, handing me a stack. "Misprints. Cheap."

Each of the twenty boxes said: "Reliance Precision Corp., Quality American Auto Farts." The guy who had taken the order on the phone must have had ears like mine.

As birds healed, we moved them from cardboard boxes to perches, where they had the freedom to exercise their wings and where they could weather, rain and sun being important to maintaining the "bloom" of their feathers, a sort of waterproofing. When a bird is weathered, the tips of the feather barbs constantly disintegrate into this talclike, water-resistant powder that gives the feather its metallic sheen.

We would have much preferred to place such birds directly into free-flight chambers in a proper mews so they could exercise as well as weather, but cage space was packed at all times. Placing them on blocks was less desirable, and we anticipated that there could be problems. There were.

We received a short-eared owl we called Stoned Owl because he had been confiscated from a "Happy House" during a drug raid. The conservation officer who had been called in to pick up the owl said the air was thick with marijuana smoke, and truly the owl seemed sleepier and wiser than most owls when we got him. He had crude jesses on, and after carefully checking him out for any injuries, Stel deemed him fit, except for broken and missing tail feathers, which we knew would moult back in rapidly if the bird was given a good diet and some peace.

Stel cut new jesses from the big piece of leather we had bought for just this purpose, and we looked around for a place to put his block perch. We settled on a spot in the bottoms near the creek, where confiscated young red-tailed and Swainson's hawks had been perched prior to release. The owl was there for several days, doing well I thought, until one morning I went down and found two feather-footed owl legs in jesses. That was all. The jesses were still attached to the leash and perch.

"Shark," said Matthew ominously as we examined the scene of the murder. In truth it was as if a shark had bitten the owl off at the legs and taken him away. There were no feathers around to indicate a struggle or that this was a killing site, so the owl must have been carried off by whatever predator had gotten him. I can only guess that a raccoon came upon him, or possibly a skunk, and killed the owl quickly, but when it tried to carry the body off and was stopped by the jesses and leash, it bit or tore the legs from the body. I looked along the stream bottom and in the nearby thickets but found not a trace of the victim. It was an eerie feeling that followed me back to the house. More than ever we realized our need for a proper mews.

Enter Al Heggen, chief of nongame, Utah Division of Wildlife Resources. John Nagel, law-enforcement chief, had turned the long-term liaison between us and the UDWR over to Heggen, a lanky, crew-cut Norwegian with a voice like a cannon: "I seem to be able to get attention and that gets things done," he once bellowed at me in his normal, hundred-decibel voice.

Heggen, a student of tortoises, was a quick read, and in a short time had become conversant with raptors and raptor problems. He soon perceived that birds of prey were highly regarded by the public, a fact that was not lost on a man just beginning to build the state's nongame wildlife program. On a late summer day Heggen called: "Can you draw up some plans for a mews?" he thundered. "I think I can get you a small grant, and maybe we can get some work and materials donated."

Is the world round? Stel and I had already worked up a set of rough plans, and we expanded them that night at the dining table after the boys were in bed. We looked at several falconry books for hints and suggestions, and finally settled on a building twenty-four feet long and twelve feet wide. At the front it would be twelve feet tall, and ten feet at the back to allow for drainage. There would be four chambers inside, each six feet wide, with each chamber running the width of the structure. Chambers would be partitioned by solid walls to keep the birds separated safely. The front and two-thirds of the top of the structure would be open, so each chamber could admit sun and rain, and this opening would be covered by one-inch strips of wood running vertically to form bars and to provide a solid-appearing wall against which birds would not bate; no wire was used in this design. Doors were planned so we could enter each chamber independently, but we really didn't think we would have room (or resources) to construct a safety chamber for each entry.

One bright, but muddy, Saturday morning a crew of trainees from the local carpenter's union tumbled out of trucks and cars as another truck delivered a load of donated lumber. Thundering hammers and raging power saws, interrupted only when Stel brought everyone in for chili, echoed through our woods until nightfall, when a mews of remarkable integrity stood ready for doors and painting. These carpentry hopefuls were *serious* about the building: it had double two-by-four reinforcement, with double nails and board-and-batten strips double secured to cover seams. "We're not keeping *elephants*," Stel whispered in awe as she looked at the strength of the construction.

A day or two later, doors were found, donated by a local lumber company. And what doors they were: four solid hardwood slabs, each elaborately scrolled and carved. Because of being a tad small, they had been rejected by the custom-home builder who had ordered them (there was probably deafness involved here somewhere). Up with the doors, designed for a hilltop mansion.

We had resolved the question of flooring material before the mews had been hammered onto the railroad-tie footings. Ideally concrete was desirable for ease of cleaning and resistance to bacterial buildup due to dampness. Our second choice was gravel, for if drained well, it would also serve as "rangle" for our birds, rangle being the grinding material birds of prey use in their gizzards to help process their food.

We were most concerned about dampness because bumblefoot, a common and usually fatal disease in birds of prey, seems to grow in dampness, and we had seen one rehabilitation project in operation that used straw on its floors and then wondered why it was having so many problems with disease. Falconers had been vocal in recommending either gravel or concrete flooring.

Concrete seemed too expensive, so gravel it would be, and Stel insisted it be rounded pea gravel from a river bottom, not sharp hillside rocks. After several calls I found a gravel company which was excavating river pebbles from Ogden's Weber River, nearly fifty miles away. "How much for gravel?" I asked.

"Fifteen bucks a truckload," said a voice.

"Great. Send me a load as soon as possible." I told him where we lived.

"That'll be $160," he said. "Delivery costs" was his only explanation.

Back to concrete. I called my brother Joe, a concrete contractor, explaining where the mews were built and what we needed. Joe patiently listened and told me it would be very, very expensive, since concrete would have to be pumped from the road down to the mews site, a distance of a hundred yards. We could not pull a truck down to the site as the creek bottoms were too soft. In past years the bottoms had flooded regularly and were layered with topsoil from centuries of cottonwood detritus. When we had built the house on higher ground, as a precaution we had installed a pump to protect the foundation from possible high water. As it turned out, the pump also kept the bottoms from becoming soggy in the spring when the creek was fed with heavy runoff from the ten-thousand-foot peaks that rose just a mile from our place. Nonetheless the ground was too soft for a big truck, Joe assured me. "Unless you want to take it down load by load in a wheelbarrow," he said, the very idea of which I rejected as I thought of aching muscles and burning lungs.

It would have to be gravel; I ordered in on Thursday, and on Saturday it was delivered while I was getting a haircut. The driver dumped the load in the middle of the driveway. Conveniently I had forgotten that gravel, like concrete, had to find its way to the mews. Thus began many hard hours spent between the handles of a wheelbarrow, with complementary aching muscles and burning lungs.

With falconer's bumblefoot warnings still in mind, we began looking for suitable perches to place in each chamber. The criteria for perches were that the bird had to have several different surfaces to supply a variety of footing, and to have enough perches in each chamber to allow it to fly to them for exercise. We placed large, natural limbs at angles and various heights; the carpenter's apprentices built some triangular corner perches that we placed near the high ceilings. Large sections of cut logs were placed on the gravel floors.

Finally we purchased large, plastic dishpans for each chamber (returning the gold pan to a grateful Matt), an additional length of hose that would carry water from the house to the mews, and heavy-duty locks for each of the doors.

The mews stood white and raw among the tall trees, and all we needed now was paint. With pride we placed our first birds in the chambers—a prairie falcon, two red-tails and an eagle, all former box residents who could now move in the capacious rooms, flapping and exercising as they flew from perch to perch.

I was uncomfortable about only one aspect of the design—the slatting had been installed horizontally rather than vertically, and I feared the birds might cling to this and damage wing or tail feathers. My concern was unwarranted, however, for never did I see a bird cling to the slats as they did to wire. I believe there is something in the psychology of the solid slatting that tells the bird it is of no use to attack the bars or try to work its way out. Wire, on the other hand, looks fragile enough to break through and may invite trouble.

There was the matter of painting now, and our jaunty painter arrived on a Wednesday morning, so I report this secondhand. Please understand that the painter is a rotund, pink-cheeked Greek. Stellanie is also Greek, so this conversation took place in Greek:

"You can't use a sprayer," said the ninety-eight-pound woman, her brown eyes flashing with anger as our painter lugged his spray gear from his truck and put on his safety mask.

"Oh yes, I can spray. I bid the job on that basis," said the painter.

"No, you can't. There are birds in there, and it will make them sick," said Stel.

"It won't make them sick," he said, waving the sprayer.

"If it won't make them sick, why are you wearing that mask?"

"It might make me sick," said the painter.

"If you get sick, the birds will get sick."

"The birds won't get sick."

"Are you telling *me* that I don't know what I'm talking about?" asked Stel. "Do you think you can push me around just because I am a woman?"

I have seen my wife angry and it is a terrible thing. The painter retreated to reconsider. He left for a while and then returned with two boys, both of whom were soon wielding paintbrushes dripping with thick, chocolate-colored outside paint. By the end of the day, the mews blended into the woods and the soil of the bottoms. We now had a palatial hawk barn.

Eagles were arriving every day. On a single day we often had an inventory of fifty birds, and sixty was not unusual. Not only had we filled all our first cages, boxes, perches and the new mews, but Stel had also found a couple of people who could become subpermittees and take a few birds into their homes.

Almost as soon as we completed the first building, we knew we needed another. One night at a party we casually asked Heggen when we were going to get our second mews. He was so pleased with the first that the second went up within months. UDWR also offered this time to paint the mews, after Heggen had heard the story of Stel's dealings with our first painter.

The painting approach this time was quite different. Assigned by UDWR to do the painting was a shy, graceful, young Navajo named Fritz Begay who had spent most of his twenty-two years on the big reservation that sprawls across southern Utah, northern Arizona and northwestern New Mexico. Fritz stepped through the door of the house that first day and just as quickly stepped back out, Stel having forgotten the Navajo superstition about owls: we happened to have a very-tame great horned owl on a perch in the kitchen. Via an emissary Fritz asked that we either cover the owl or take it elsewhere before he came back. This we did.

Fritz would work hard at the painting for an hour or two; then he would sit back on the bench in front of the mews and talk to the eagles, whittling little gifts for them, watching the forest dwellers and listening to the creek. Then he would paint hard for an hour or two. Then he might nap. I *did* admire his style. The painting took a little longer, but the job was better, we were happier and the birds, I know, were happier. Quite a contrast to our first painter who had wanted to fly through the job in an hour. Fritz later became a conservation officer with UDWR and is known for his excellent work with animals—except owls.

My one regret, I thought one day as a red-tail shot out the mews door and disappeared above the tree canopy, was that we had not built a safety chamber for each section. A hawk in captivity may wait with cunning until that moment when you least expect it, and *whish*, away he goes over your head as you open the door. We lost three or four birds that way.

The birds that escaped were always birds in good health and often were being held as court cases. There is something ironically cosmic about the escape of a bird that is being deprived of freedom so human justice can be meted out.

Flim Flam, three ounces of flammulated owl took up residence in the master bedroom. (Photo by Stellanie Ure)

7

HOUSEHOLDING WITH HAWKS

*Happy is the house that shelters
a friend.*

—RALPH WALDO EMERSON

James Thurber once wrote a story about a man who kept hearing a seal in his bedroom. When I awakened one morning, my eyes were thick with sleep and my body was disinclined to move at all. To fool the morning and the forthcoming demands of the day, I slowly lifted one eyelid; I would defy dawn by keeping the other shut. My shut eye opened abruptly, however, when I saw an owl peering up at me from inside my hiking boot, which sat on the floor next to the foot of the bed. Am I dreaming, or am I living a Thurber story? I wondered as I shook my head. The owl still sat in my boot, her yellow eyes looking directly at me. She was not your typical owl, but the only owl in North America that lives in the ground—a burrowing owl— and she apparently thought my boot was a burrow, or at least a hidey-hole. We called this owl Strider.

I was waking to many new birds in the house these days, since all our outside mews and all our cages were still unable to handle the spillover of birds. After several weeks of treatment in a box, a bird would either be placed on a perch where it could bate for exercise, or as space became available, Stel would transfer it to the mews. Some birds could stay in the house, depending on how they eliminated their feces, called mutes.

The mutes of falcons and owls drop straight down into tidy piles around the base of the perch. But goshawks, Cooper's hawks, sharp-shins, red-tails, ferruginous hawks, rough-legged hawks and eagles all "slice" when they mute; that is, they throw the mute back and away in a stream, sometimes shooting it six feet or more. Droppers were easy to clean up after, slicers were not; so slicers usually went outdoors and droppers were kept in the house.

Our house had been designed and sited for us in the cotton-woods by John Sugden, a colleague of Mies van der Rohe, and the architecture reflected the spare, open approach of Mies. The house was forty-four feet by forty-four feet, and its exterior walls were constructed of eleven-by-eleven-foot panels of lightly bronzed glass set into Corten steel frames. Its floor plan was flexible and partitions were movable, designed around a core of utilities, with bathrooms and kitchen at the center of the house. We configured the house so that the front was an open space twenty-two feet by forty-four feet, which served as a living room-dining room; the master bedroom was behind it on one side, the boys' bedrooms on the other.

Strider the burrowing owl was a dropper and would eventually have the run of the house, unperched, unboxed, free to travel wherever she would, even at the risk of tangling with the other birds jessed and leashed to inside perches. Strider was the second burrowing owl we had had; the first had had an irreparable foot injury and had gone to a local zoo. Strider came to us covered with oil, and Cory and Stel laboriously removed it over a period of several days with cotton swabs, mineral oil and cornstarch. The owl had been oiled when some heavy equipment had been drained at the site of her burrow, and she was the only survivor of her nestmates, all of which had drowned in the thick tractor oil which flooded their underground den.

Strider was the size of a large Idaho potato, and she could set off on a long-legged sprint at surprising speed. It was on one of the first days she was with us that I awoke to see her sitting in my boot. She shot under the bed in a twinkling. I was certain that the night before she had been secure in a cardboard box.

Stel and I peered under the bed at the leggy owl: "Well, she got out," said Stel, shaking her head. Sure enough, Strider had managed to enlarge a hole in her cardboard box, an unusual occurrence. I had figured the bird would be too subdued for anything after looking at her sorry, soiled state. That morning she was quite lively, thank you, sprinting through our bedroom a darn sight faster than I could run. Strider's little feet beat a muffled *pat-pat-pat-pat-pat* as she raced across the carpet and dashed into the flotsam and jetsam of my closet. It was clear she felt safe in dark places.

We closed the bedroom door to keep her contained, but decided to let her have the run of the room for now; we had a prairie falcon, a great horned owl and a couple of kestrels tied to perches elsewhere in the house, and they could be of great danger to her. A couple of days passed, however, and we decided to open the bedroom door, although we were ready to spring to her aid as the little runner cautiously explored the rest of the house. She stood back from the prairie falcon, emitted two quailing little sounds of fear and dashed back to the bedroom. It was immediately apparent that Strider was perfectly capable of avoiding the perched birds that might be dangerous to her. From then on, Strider moved about the house freely, part of the family, living much like a house cat might.

Burrowers are unusual in the world of owls. They nest in open fields and deserts at the ends of tunnels usually previously occupied by prairie dogs, badgers or coyotes. They can and do create burrows of their own (I giggle at the image of an owl tossing dirt out behind itself like a digging puppy). Burrowers are only slightly larger than the common, woods-dwelling screech owl, but look larger because they stand straight and tall on long legs that would be envied by any show girl.

You may see them in the wild at the lip of their burrows, where they lay up to ten eggs in a clutch. Burrowers often begin a comical head bobbing when alarmed or approached, and while they look sort of knock-kneed and awkward, they are not ungainly at all. I am positive they could run down their quarry on foot, yet they are powerful flyers and unlike other owls, they have a swift, "birdy" wing beat similar to that of kestrels. Males weigh about seven ounces, females somewhat more, in keeping with the reverse dimorphism in raptors previously mentioned. They have a wingspan of about two feet.

As with other owls, burrowers have asymmetrical ear cavities and an auditory sense so acute they can hear even the flight of a beetle or a grasshopper at a considerable distance.

We began to understand the colonial nature of the bird as we spent more time observing her. Burrowers historically have inhabited some very large colonies throughout the West, and living together provides them with a good strategy for survival. They have large clutches of eggs, which may help offset the losses that a ground-dwelling bird expects from skunks, weasels, large snakes, badgers, ferrets and other hawks and falcons.

Burrowers in northern Utah are declining, primarily because of the nesting land being taken up by housing and industry. Where I used to see burrowers on the sagebrush flats west of Salt Lake City, I now see concrete tilt-slab buildings and mile after mile of housing subdivisions. Burrowers seem to be somewhat adaptable, for they have been known to take up residence in drains in cities, and have been seen flying around city streetlights capturing moths (mostly they eat mice, rats, insects and some small birds). They have the unusual owl habit of collecting oddments in their burrows, including bits of charcoal, fragments of colored rags, lost mittens, corncobs, and quite frequently, cow dung.

The owl books told me they were crepuscular—or most active mornings and evenings, which was certainly true of our Strider.

Strider would busy about in the morning, watching Cory's breakfast preparations with apparent bemusement from the counter as he mixed his secret-recipe hotcake batter, the ingredients of which only he and Strider knew.

During the day Strider rested on the floor, looking through the glass walls at the activity in the woods. During winter she quickly learned that the floor vents sent heat billowing up into her breast and belly, warming her as she stood atop the vent on one leg, eyes dreamily half shut, great eyelashes slowly blinking. In fact, at the sound of the furnace clicking on, she would race to the nearest heating vent to await the luxurious flow of heat. (My own observations lead me to believe that many animals seek such warmth, perhaps in order to conserve their own heat and thus slow their metabolic rate that would normally require more food, and therefore more hunting.)

When Stel and I turned off the television set or closed our books and prepared to go to bed, Strider would immediately head for our bedroom, where she would jump into her roosting box for the night. In the morning she would go into either Cory's or Matt's room and *gritch* them awake with her squeaky greeting. Stel and I always knew where she was by the sound of whichever son's voice was talking to her.

Then she would fly out to greet me with a morning *gritch* as I made coffee. She sat on the counter, comfortably settled on one leg in my sleepy-eyed company, and patiently waited for Stel to thaw her a mouse or a chicken thigh, occasionally calling for Cory or Matt to get up, get up.

Burrowers do not hoot; Strider made a variety of sounds, usually her soft *gritch*, sometimes a *kak-kak-kak-kak!* when alarmed, or a tiny, throaty trill when she was fed or warm, or sometimes a sound like a cuckoo clock. Her most amazing sound came one day when Strider spied a golden eagle on which Stellanie was working. The little owl focused fixedly on her natural enemy and shrieked a harsh, rattling, almost-hysterical roar. Later research disclosed an interesting fact: burrowers make a sound very much like a rattlesnake when humans or another predator attempt to dig into their burrows. The sound would sure as hell dissuade me.[5]

Heggen, now visiting our home regularly, fell in love with Strider, and the little bird was instrumental in establishing the first artificial nesting boxes for owl colonies in our area. Heggen, after falling under Strider's spell, arranged with our local power company to construct burrows to encourage burrower breeding along the power-line rights-of-way in north-central Utah.

Strider also learned to return to her box when the hustle and bustle of household activity and visitors and children became too great. She would utter her best *coo-coo* and dash for her box, a dark closet or my boot, knock-knees and long legs propelling her at flank speed, a disconcerting image when one thinks in conventional-owl terms.

Life in my bedroom was soon composed of the sounds of cuckoos, rattlesnakes and the patter of little feet, and we anxiously awaited Strider's first moult in the belief that new plumage would allow her to be freed to the wild. I must say that we had conflicting emotions when her first moult came, and her new feathers came in strangely twisted and curled, the feather ducts apparently having been somehow damaged either by trauma or stress during her initial oiling. We loved her as part of the family, yet knew the bird deserved her freedom. We waited year after year, watching each moult carefully, but Strider was never able to go free. Stel continued to lovingly follow Strider's trail through the house at the end of each day, wiping her whitewash from carpets, vents and counters.

Late one evening a well-dressed man arrived at our door carrying a shoe box. A small owl had caromed off his windshield in the Federal Heights area of Salt Lake City, and after no-little effort on his part to find a place for it, he had found us.

"Is it a baby?" he asked, unbuttoning his camel-hair sport coat as he leaned over the box while Stel gently felt the fierce-eyed little creature, who looked up with challenging fury at all of us.

"It's a pygmy owl," said Stel with the delight in her voice that she reserves for things small and soft and precious.

The tiny bird had a reputation for fierceness in spite of its size, which in this case we guessed may have been only two ounces, for he was slender. His miniature, horn-colored beak clicked like a fishing reel, and his small round eyes with their yellow irises gave him a look not of fear, but of angry indignance, as if to say, "Have you no respect?"

His wing was dragging and obviously broken, and Stel did not know if it would mend. I made the necessary cuts in a small box and placed a rock inside as a perch for Pepita, whose name came at that moment because he was no bigger, said Stel, than a pumpkinseed. Stel continued to examine the bird as we leaned over him like a football huddle. When Pepita turned, the feathering on the back of his head and neck took on the appearance of another set of eyes and a beak. We had seen a hint of this in other owls, but none so pronounced as in this angry shrimp. It looked like a second face, and we speculated that it was a means of warding off possible enemies, or of keeping the niggling passerines that constantly harass little owls at a distance. I had read accounts of flocking jays pecking pygmy owls to death. Perhaps this second face kept them at a distance.

I cannot imagine a right-minded bird attacking a pygmy owl (except for my great horned owls, which I love dearly yet still find demented). There is a record of a pygmy owl catching and killing a "larger-than-average chicken." It is known to regularly kill birds and mammals twice its size.[6]

We were so absorbed with our new guest that we had forgotten the man who had brought him until he bid adieu, after first offering to leave money for the care of the owl. Stel thanked him and told him that would not be necessary, though I was now beginning to wonder. Food costs were becoming a big consideration as our bird load increased.

The next day the little owl ate some chicken as he sat on a rock in the bottom of his box in our bedroom, looking up at us with his little pearl eyes, and clacking his beak rapidly and fiercely, as if daring us to come nearer.

Now that Matthew had his gold pan back, he was once again hard at ore recovery. We had made a short trip to the Comstock Lode in Virginia City, Nevada, where he had acquired an antique miner's lamp and an old-fashioned miner's hard hat, which one evening he was wearing as he panned gravel in the bathtub in the master bathroom. Suddenly a tiny bird jumped from the floor to land with a splash in the bathtub, where it materialized into a soggy and defiant Pepita pygmy owl, shaking and dipping as he bathed in the tub, his wing hanging but obviously of some use. He had chewed a hole in his cardboard box with that tiny, strong beak, and was obliviously splish-splashing. Hearing Matt's roar of delight, we all ran to the bathroom, where Stel quickly closed the door to make certain the owl was confined, fearful that Strider or one of the other birds might get him (we were yet to realize that Pepita might be of more danger to one of *them*).

His bath finished, Pepita now flew to the flat base of a table lamp and, warmed by the glow of the bulb, dried himself over the next hour, preening his tail, wings and back feathers methodically, but ever watchful. I imagined how comfortable the little bird, hurt and captive, must have been as he sat in the warmth of the light, clean for the first time in many days.

After putting Pepita back in his box (and noticing for the first time how unusually strong and warm his small feet were), I returned to the comfort of my sofa to watch Cory practicing his magic tricks, since he was now a partner in a corporation, consisting of himself and his friend Tony Keyser, called The Black Hat Magicians. He and

Tony had several business ventures, including C&T Wood Enter-prises, which sold cut-up dead wood from our property and was famous for once netting eighty dollars on a single sale. The new venture—magic shows for birthdays and other parties—promised to be even more lucrative, said Cory, waving a wand over a deck of cards.

A strange sound drifted in from the bedroom: it was a soft trill, followed by a slow *tink . . . tink . . . tink*. The source of the sound was Pepita's box. I turned to the *Life Histories of North American Birds of Prey* by Arthur Cleveland Bent to see what descriptions there were of the vocalizations of pygmy owls. These are always amusing, since people describe bird sounds in so many different ways. The three descriptions in Bent were: *0-0-0-0-0-0-0-0-0-0-0-0-0-0-0————0-0;* and *too-too-too-too-too-too-too*; and *toot-toot-toot-toot-toot*. A fourth description was *(si) poolk (ngh)*. Bent went on to say, "It may be best imitated by a whistle which is conscientiously modified by atten-dant grimaces."[7]

Do we hear things differently from species to species? For comparison I looked up the "voice" for long-eared owls in the same book. The sounds ascribed to them were *whoof-whoof-whoof, wuck-wuck-wuck, wek-wek-wek,* or *mie-e-ew, mie-e-ew.*

This of course got me going on the old naturalists and the wonderful descriptions of birds that have come down to us from the nineteenth and early-twentieth centuries, and how they point out that each human may hear and describe the sound differently. I fingered the pages of the book, delighted at how precise the descrip-tions attempted to be, lacking as they were the media that today can show us how birds look (television, video recordings, and easily portable, color photographic equipment for field use). To describe the coloring of peregrine eggs, the old-time naturalists used "Mo-rocco red," "Kaiser brown," "cinnamon rufous," and "pallid purple drab." Terms like "vinaceous russet," "sepia" and "bister" were used to describe the colors of a kestrel in the old books. Today's students of nature would delight in reading some of these aging tomes. I reflected on how the natural sciences today are loaded with technicians; scholars with a larger view abound in the old works. I closed Bent and went to bed at a late hour.

Pepita now had complete charge of the upper half of our bed-room, as our patch job on his box had lasted only a hour before the little fury flew to the headboard of our bed and claimed his territory there. As with Strider, any commotion would send him flying back into the darkness and safety of his box, the equivalent of his nest hole, and like Strider, he was active morning and evening, with long periods of napping in between. He usually sat quietly under the lamp, or on top of the faucet in the bathroom sink where he blended into the fitting, much to the discomfort of a female guest who decided to wash her hands. At night he mostly stayed in his box, sitting on his rock.

There was a sense of calm that reigned over the birds of the house, and we were not really surprised when Strider and Pepita peacefully divvied up the bedroom territory, Strider taking the floor, Pepita finding space at about waist level, either on the headboard or in the bathroom. Strider's wanderings encompassed the entire house; Pepita seldom left our bedroom or bathroom, so shy was he. We were very careful at first to see if one of them might attack the other, but it never happened. They ignored each other completely.

It was one thing to have a pygmy owl living in the house, but we were presented with entirely new problems when we received a four-to-five-week-old golden eagle, which like the three-hundred-pound boy inevitably called Tiny, we named Baby. Baby, her head sprouting sprightly little flags of down, had been "found" in the Escalante desert of southern Utah and was brought to us by one of our friends with the UDWR, Mike Coffeen, who worked out of Cedar City. She was slicing in apparent good health, and we surmised that whoever had taken her from the nest must not have had her very long, or had treated her very well.

I gathered nest material as Stel made a box up for the young eagle. Snippets of pine, and pencil-sized twigs were placed in the bottom of a large cardboard box, providing an aromatic nest into which Stellanie lowered the young eagle, being exceptionally careful of her feet—even at this age they can exert pressure at something like five hundred pounds per square inch. Such talons can crush the bones in a large jackrabbit, or in a human hand, even an arm. We had heard of cases of eagles killing their human handlers in Russia. Our concerns about having the eaglet in the house were not so much for ourselves or the boys, who were bird wise now, but for neighbor children who roared through the house with Cory, riding imaginary motorcycles with six-guns blazing (a mixed metaphor which surely must be some kind of statement about the last decades of the twentieth century in the West).

Stel had Baby eating in just minutes, by stroking her feet with some chicken, an act which often stimulates a raptor to feed once it is past its initial fear. Within a day the youngster was chirping with anticipation as Stel opened her box, holding a dead rat or three or four mice purchased from a pet shop at pirate's prices.

Stel sat with the young eagle for up to four hours a day, talking and playing with her, and throwing sticks a few inches, watched carefully by the eaglet. "There is something going on in that bird's head," said Stellanie one evening. "She is thinking. She watches my moves, and she can anticipate what I am going to do with the stick by moving to the edge of the box where she can pick it up after I toss it."

Within two weeks Baby was rich brown with the darkest, longest, most chocolatey feathers she would ever have, and a streamlined helmet of brassy gold. Young eagle plumage is almost black, and because they need the additional wing-and-tail loading for buoyancy and maneuvering as they learn to fly, their feathers are half an inch or so longer during their first year. As she aged and moulted, Baby's feathers would become shorter and lighter in color, until in old age she may literally have a lot of pale gray in her earthen-colored plumage.

The inevitable happened one day when Baby exercised her way out of the box. I was at the office, the boys were in school, and Stel sat on the bed to try to figure out the best approach. Baby was by now very familiar with Stel and used to having her provide meals as well as diversion. She strutted across the carpet and gently jumped up on the bed, right on Stel's knee, where the eagle precariously teetered as Stel held her breath. The first reaction of any teetering bird is to grip, which is what she now did to Stel's knee. Stel relaxed as Baby composed herself and ruffled her wings and tail feathers, comfortably perched with a firm but gentle pressure.

Baby sat expectantly, waiting for Stel to give her a mouse, while Stel dared not move for fear of invoking the inevitable clinging grip. As the Great Hawk would have it, Baby's attention was fixed on the clunking and clicking of our digital clock radio, its technology having gone bonkers so long ago that we had become accustomed to it. She stepped off to have a closer look, and then was distracted by the peperomia plant. Stel was able to go to the kitchen for a mouse, which Baby dutifully followed into her box with a chortling whistle of pursuit.

My turn next: a Saturday morning and I was sleeping in. I lay in bed vaguely aware the rest of the family was up. I heard a thump from Baby's box, and a moment later felt Baby working her way, one foot slowly ahead of the other, up my leg. It is an ominous sensation to have an eagle walking on you, since they weigh considerably more than any hawk. Even young birds have talons the size of bear claws. I, too, was aware that any quick movement would result in a sturdy grip on the object underfoot, which now happened to be my thigh. Wasn't the femoral artery right there somewhere? Baby began chirping and chortling as she headed, via me, for the peperomia. At my chest she stopped and looked me in the face, as if to say, "Just passing through."

"Stel," I called. "It's time for Baby to go into the mews." Stel later told me I sounded calm.

The move to the mews required a certain logistical strategy. Stellanie did not want Baby to associate the discomfort of being handled by humans with her, since birds of prey are able to discern between individual humans and know the ones they do not trust. Baby would likely someday go to a breeding project, and Stel would have to continue to work with the bird. Stel wanted all the goodwill she could retain.

So we asked our good friend and an accomplished falconer, Steve Chindgren, to assist. Chindgren arrived, thick muscular legs and arms straining against his shorts and T-shirt. His physique had been acquired through years of training hawks and chasing them through the most rugged terrain. I have seen Steve run five miles at full speed to "make into" a gyrfalcon that has flown down a sage grouse. His talents as a trainer are legendary and almost every year he wins the North American Falconer's Association meet with his fine-tuned falcons. Chindgren at this time had not worked with eagles, and he said he was curious and willing to help.

The first step was to jess the eaglet. Talking all the while, Stel reached over Baby's back as she stood in her box, taking hold of both her legs very firmly. Baby was scarcely aroused, so used was she to Stel by now. Stel carried Baby to a chair and sat in it, the bird on her lap. Baby promptly began nibbling at the shiny buttons on Stel's shirt, then turned her attention to the dangling earrings she wore. Steve, meanwhile, quickly fit the leather bracelets around Baby's legs, snapping them in place with pop rivets. These were aylmeri jesses, designed so a bird could pull the loose leather straps free should it escape, a good precaution that prevents a bird from getting the leather lines caught in something. Many escaped trained falcons have died when their straight-line jesses got twisted on a branch, suspending the bird until it suffocated. With aylmeri jesses, the bird can preen them out, often within an hour of escape. This makes the bird harder to recover but saves its life if it returns to the wild, as many falconers' birds do.

The jesses on, Steve then pulled on a leather glove. "She can sit on my fist and I'll carry her to the mews, like a falcon," Steve said, adding that he believed the light falconer's glove would be adequate.

Baby stepped onto his fist, and being unsure of this new surface, of course gripped with all her strength. We heard the bones in Steve's hand cracking ominously, and Stel quickly placed a thick branch behind the eaglet's feet. When a raptor feels a surface behind its tarsi like this, it always steps backward onto the new surface.

Steve's hand was released, and he expelled his breath with relief.

Baby rode heroically on the branch now held by Stel. In a moment she was in her new mews, looking up as if to say, "Now what was that all about?" Steve's later X ray showed a series of hairline fractures in the bones of his wrist.

Baby was everyone's favorite. Each day we would go to the mews to play "sticks" with her. She pounced on a tossed stick and would offer it back, holding her head low and turning it on one side as eyas (young) birds do. Baby became something of a crowd pleaser.

She attracted a number of visitors, including actress Katharine Ross, whom I had met in the course of some work. She was in town to judge and be part of a film festival with the glitterati, to ride horses with Robert Redford, and as it turned out, to fly falcons with Steve Chindgren and I. She came to the house where we had lunch, then Stel took her to the mews where Baby proceeded to put on a show: chirping, playing sticks, and allowing Katharine to scratch her head and feathered feet, something Baby seldom did with strangers. Stel speculated the bird reacted this way because she and Katharine were approximately the same height and had similar coloring. Katharine was enchanted by our raptors and asked if she might sometime go flying falcons.

The next day Steve and I took Katharine hawking near Great Salt Lake. It was raining and Steve made her work to help flush the game for his gyrfalcon. When the morning ended, she was rosy cheeked and laughing hard, and her lovely bronze hair was hanging in wet tendrils across her face. When Katharine left two days later, she announced that the best part of her trip had been scratching an eagle's head.

Baby had imprinted on Stel, a psychobiological process whereby the young bird basically attaches itself to its handler for food, security and affection. Since Baby had been a few weeks old when taken by humans, she knew she was a bird. Very young birds taken and placed with people reach a degree of imprinting where they become extremely tame and easily handled, perhaps because they really do not discern any difference between themselves and the humans that have raised them.

Imprinting makes for great pets, but we could not lose sight of the fact that we were in business not to have bird friends, but to release birds back to the wild. At the time many biologists and falconers said imprinted birds could not be released to the wild since they would turn to the nearest human for food and attention, and that would likely result in a shotgun blast and a dead bird. Eagles especially are a release problem. Fran Hammerstrom had to drive from her home in Wisconsin to the desolate badlands of Wyoming before letting her imprinted eagle go.

An imprinted eagle, if released near humans, will likely fly to the nearest person for food. I sometimes imagined, for instance, the Swenson family reunion, at which a recently released Baby would float from the sky to settle gently among the potato salad and pickles, then adroitly crush the terrified family's roasted chicken with her massive beak, one huge foot holding down its stern.

Imprinting had created a concern about Baby's future until I heard about the prospects of her going to a breeding project, which often utilizes tame birds. The search for a home for Baby finally settled on a project in Illinois run by a man named Bill Voelker. Voelker prepared eagles for reintroduction and was also keeper of feathers for the Comanche tribe. Proper permits were obtained, and soon it was time for Baby to leave.

For purely sentimental reasons, Stel did not want to have to handle Baby—to package and ship her. Once again Chindgren was called upon, and again he gladly volunteered help, and again Baby crunched him, this time higher on the arm, leaving great purple bruises that took weeks to heal. Steve packaged Baby, her brown eye looking accusingly at Stel through a hole in the shipping crate. Stel supervised the loading of the bird on the Delta Air Lines jet, including explicit, oft-repeated instructions on handling, water, and delivery at the other end.

With a chirp and a chortle, Baby disappeared into the cargo hold of the jet. A few hours later, a tearful Stel bit her lip and fingered the peperomia as a phone call from Voelker announced Baby's safe arrival.

The daintiest, most elegant of all the North American falcons was a decided counterpoint to Baby, but as Emerson said, "I think no virtue goes with size." We called her Muscles, for reasons I suppose were similar to those used in naming Baby. Muscles was one of the tiniest, darkest kestrels we ever received: delicate looking; finely marked with dark teardrop malers below each eye; each feather intricately simple, with scallops of blackest black against umber. Muscles started with us in a box, and became the darling of the boys since they were assigned to watch and feed her. Within a short time Muscles was jessed and placed on a tiny bow perch in the living room. We quickly saw what an amiable bird she was, and after encouragement from Cory one afternoon, Stel locked Strider in the bedroom and released Muscles so she could fly about freely in the front part of the house. Shortly thereafter it became apparent that, like the relationship—or rather, lack of it—between the burrower and the pygmy owl, Muscles had found her own niche at a higher level in the house, and chose to spend much of her time on one of the overhead beams, completely ignoring Strider on the floor, steering clear of a prairie falcon perched in a corner, and giving a wide berth to Tufter, the puppylike great horned owl who was so tame he came to your lap to be petted.

Muscles was thoroughly curious and equally courageous, and often we would come rushing to the living room in response to the ruckus of an angry perched bird whose dinner (or leftovers) had just been stolen by Muscles in a sneak attack from the beam. Falcons will stash their leftovers, and Muscles was no exception. She liked best to keep her half-mouse snack "for later" by storing it on a heating vent in the floor.

By now she had taken a liking to the top of the kitchen cabinets near the warm lights, and from there she might flutter down to land on my fist as I sliced beef for teriyaki for our dinner. Once she descended on a rat five times her size being prepared for an eagle in the mews. Often she would land in a house plant, nibble at its leaves, then contentedly snooze in the greenery, all but impossible to see until we got used to her habits.

But bring a strange new bird into the house—especially an eagle or an owl—and Muscles would set up a frenzied alarm call, *kee-kee-kee-kee-kee*, to be joined by Strider, alerted by the kestrel, who would break into a terrifying snakelike *hasssssssssh*.

Muscles flitted from beam to beam, plant to plant, and Stellanie wishfully encouraged the little bird to fly through the ceiling cobwebs as an aid to housecleaning.

Muscles brought me a most ignominious moment one morning as I climbed from the shower, having left the bathroom door open. We were regularly feeding chicken necks to the kestrels of the house, and she attacked what she apparently thought was just another chicken neck. Unfortunately it was still attached to its owner—me. Thereafter I closed the bathroom door. And that's the truth.

Piwacket the magpie drinks water from Matthew's mouth. Magpies were one of many non-raptors that found their way into the project. (Photo by Stellanie Ure)

8
Ravens, Pigeons and Pipits

*The devil must be in that little
jackdaw.*
—Richard Harris Barham

When birds made their way into the house, invariably they made their way into our hearts; and house birds were not always restricted to raptors. As inevitably as daffodils in March, we received some nonraptors that we did not have the heart to turn away.

One of the falconers, knowing how difficult it often was for us to obtain proper food, brought us a pigeon one morning. He offered to kill it, but after Stel looked in the box at the blue-barred common pigeon and was greeted by a gentle *peep* and a low *hooo,* she made a silent decision that the bird would not become food. The pigeon's wattles (the skin around the beak) were smooth and undeveloped, and its feathers were still soft and growing, sure signs that the bird was just barely fledged.

"I'll take care of it," she said to the departing falconer, more of whom were spending symbiotic time with us. Any falconer is bound to be a certifiable bird junkie, and all our hawks gave them a chance to drink in an abundance of raptors for comparison against their experiences and information. Falconers early on helped us to see subtle differences in birds, and Stel in turn was able to provide them with data on bird health and physiology that they had no access to, and that few veterinarians anywhere had had an opportunity to learn, chickens being considered the only bird worthy of economic consideration at the time.

Stel placed the bird and its box next to the dining room table, near the fireplace, and put in a small pan of grain and a small bowl of water. For several days she only fed and watered the bird and could otherwise give it little attention, but this was all the time it took for the bird to become thoroughly conditioned to the arrival of food and water at the appearance of Stel's face over the top of the box. Soon it was clear that the pigeon—named Homer by Cory—was imprinted. Each time Stel opened the box, Homer cooed, flipped her wings gently and dipped her head coyly.

"We are in the hawk business," I reminded her. But she got me at point-blank range when she asked me for alternatives to keeping the bird. Find some pigeon fancier? They wanted no common pigeons. Downtown the Jaycees were shooting pigeons as a civic project, and the city fathers were poisoning them. "Perhaps an unsuspecting child will come along and we can give Homer to him," I suggested hopefully.

The boys began letting Homer out of her box. Neither the two small owls—Strider and Pepita—nor the kestrel now at large offered any threat to the pigeon, but we took extra care, since we expected she was a bird of little brain and might wander too close to one of the large birds on perches. Not to worry. Homer preferred to move on foot, and Homer stayed very close to the dining room table. She could be readily picked up and returned to her box, cooing with affection as she felt herself gathered within warm human hands.

"Maybe it's time to fly her at hack," I suggested one day. Flying at hack is a falconer's term for allowing a young falcon or a semitrained falcon to fly at will, yet keeping it within easy trapping range by providing food for it at a "hack station" each day. In the old days this allowed young birds to really learn to fly, yet kept them close so they could be taken up in the autumn when serious training and hunting took place.

Thereafter I would pick Homer out of her box each morning as the coffee perked in the pot, and then I would open the door and let Homer launch from my hand into the dawn. Most days she balanced for a moment on my open palm, perhaps leaving a small offering as birds do to minimize flight weight, then lifted off for a short outing through the woods. We realized there were goshawks and other raptors living wild in the neighborhood, but Homer had to take risks with her life as do all living things—or else it's not much of a life.

During the day Homer visited our neighbors, flying down to the Keyser's to feed with their hens, or over to McClure's to pick at bits of gravel in their driveway. Sometimes she would sit on our roof quietly and contentedly for long periods. Other times she would come to the door and stand by it until one of us opened it so she could come in.

At sunset Homer would appear at the door, and in she would walk, slowly but confidently, greeting us with small cries and coos as she made her way to her box. She would jump in the box, eat and drink, then nap for a while. After dinner she would come out of her box and join the boys at the fireplace, cooing and wing flipping, or sitting quietly as she preened.

It was a fine parlor trick for guests when Stel said, "Lights out, Homer." The bird promptly jumped into her box, settled on the floor, dipping her head in coos and calls, and set in for the night as Stel closed her securely in the box. (It was for her own good. We worried about one of our perched hawks or owls getting loose at night and getting Homer.)

Concern for our loving *columbiforme* caused us a lot of consternation one night when she failed to return. The boys called for her around the area, but no Homer responded. There were increasingly anxious sounds from the boys as the night grew dark and the raccoons and great horned owls began their evening prowls. They went to bed fearful for their Homer. Guess who greeted me at the door the next morning? The silly pigeon ambled past me as I slid the door open, then jumped into her box to feed hungrily. How do you tell a pigeon you were worried?

We had always thought Homer was a female, and sadly found out with certainty when she languished and one morning we found her dead in her box. She had become egg bound, and there was nothing we were finally able to do for her except make her comfortable. She was with us for more than a year.

The story of Peep ends happily, however. Peep came to us as what falconers call an "LBB," or "little brown bird," species unknown. The bird had come from Cecret Lake near Alta (Cecret being the spelling of a nineteenth-century miner who had registered silver claims on the lake which was in Little Cottonwood Canyon a few miles southeast of us).

This bird was downy, tan with dark brown spots and stripes, and had inordinately long legs. We had no idea what it was, so formulating a proper diet for this baby was hit-and-miss. Diet in birds is *everything*, especially for a sensitive, growing nestling, and Stel had to guess at its needs. Its beak told us a lot—it looked like an insect eater. The survival of this bird seemed like a long shot.

Stel boiled an egg and grated the yolk, then added a dash of calcium tablet, a bit of grated apple, some uncooked Cream of Wheat, and a bit of ground beef for animal protein. She mixed this into a paste, then offered a bite of it to the little bird on the end of a toothpick. Surprise: the little peeper hungrily gobbled the mixture, eating till it was full. Stel then prepared Peep a box, placing it atop a heating pad set on low.

We were planning a long weekend fishing in Wyoming and we had not counted on a baby bird with a feeding schedule which had intervals of only a few hours. A friend was going to stop by to take care of the hawks, owls and eagles in the house and in the mews, but Peep was a problem. It wasn't fair to saddle our friend with an unknown bird on a diet that required frequent feedings.

"We'll take it with us," said Stel firmly. And we did. Peep accompanied us into restaurants, got a grand view of the Tetons and the Snake River, went fishing and bird watching, and at night was kept comfortable in the motel next to the bed on a heating pad. She was not only well; she was thriving when we completed our thousand-mile journey.

We did not have long to wait to find out what our bird was, although it occurred almost by default and not through any knowledge of our own. Peep's feathers were now completely in, and she was ready to fledge. We got the little chick up on the table with our bird books spread out, looking carefully at her shape, her eyes, her feet, the beak, the wing bars—all the field marks that birders look for. I looked at bird after bird, discarding one after another, muttering that I was a raptor person, not an LBB person.

Steve Chindgren stopped for a visit that morning, looked down at the bird and all my books, then said matter-of-factly: "Oh. When did you get a water pipit?" A water pipit! We could release the bird in our own backyard and she would be in suitable habitat. Next day we took Peep in her box to the patio, bade her good-bye, and opened the box. Peep looked up and as if she were perfectly aware it was time to go, made a couple of tiny sounds as she looked at us; then gathering her legs under her, she launched off the box edge and buzzed off toward the creek as if she had been flying for years.

Strangely she never seemed to imprint on us, in spite of handling and closeness that would have created a strong bond with any raptor and most songbirds. This is a curious matter that leads me to wonder what part of imprinting may be pure biology, and what part behavioral, and how bird species differ in their responses as shaped by these factors.

Send in the clowns! If I only have one life to live as a bird, let me live it as a raven.

Chiquita the raven got her name from the banana box in which she arrived. She was fully grown, and her primary feathers had been cut to prevent her from flying. Obviously raised by humans from an early age—likely even a downy nestling—Chiquita was a total imprint, loving and well adjusted to humans. She was fat, indicating she had been well cared for, unlike the other two ravens that had come to us.

The first raven we called Wild Biter, which about summarizes her temperament. She had been pinioned—that is, her wing had been amputated at the carpal joint to prevent her from flying, a painful and irreversible operation that likely was done without anesthetic, what with the cost of veterinary care. Her feather condition indicated she had been kept in a small, damaging cage. Her nasty disposition was predictable, and after some work by Stel and the kids, the bird mellowed out a tad. In his infinite wisdom, a certain wildlife worker dictated that we give Wild Biter to a petting zoo, where I understand she has terrorized the children evermore.

The second raven we received was brought to us as a very young downy, its eyes barely open. "Hi," said the tall, red-bearded falconer who presented the bird, complete with a half-finished can of cat food and a tongue depressor used as a spoon. "I got this raven for my girlfriend, but she's afraid of it. Will you take it?"

The man took me out to his truck in which sat a large springer spaniel and a big adult goshawk, its red eye flashing with accipiter lightning. Another flighty goshawk, I thought, and was promptly proved wrong as the bird gently reached over and began preening the falconer's hair and nibbling his ear.

"I've had Gos eight years and in that same time I've had four wives and a girlfriend. Only the bird is still with me," he said more to himself than to me, reflecting on his way with birds and lack thereof with women. He left us the raven and in the process borrowed a pair of binoculars, which must have gone the way of his wives, for I've yet to see them again.

We named this raven Marven (with an e) Raven and he was raised during a time of very heavy bird load. Consequently we never got to know this raven well, nor was he very imprinted, and he was released at about eight weeks of age at Farmington Bay at the same time we released a prairie falcon.

Chiquita was a different case. She knew and loved humans, and we delighted in her as we kept her through her moult with every intention of releasing her when her feathers grew back in. Chickie could fly twenty-five or thirty feet with laborious pumping, but could not possibly make it in the wild with her primaries cut off the way they were. At first we kept her in the house in a box, but after it became clear that she had thoroughly enchanted the boys and had them coming to her every *quork* and *gaak*, it was decided to take her outside and let her begin flying at hack.

Her innocent vandalism started quietly enough when she shredded my morning newspaper the first day out. Birds will be birds, ho-ho, I thought as I drove the mile down the lane to the convenience store for another paper. When I returned, she was amusing herself by conversing with the golden eagles in the mews, talking deep in her throat. It was like a combination of growling and chuckling, and it infected all of us with the giggles whenever she would appear and begin her articulations while cocking her head, and anticipating our responses as if she clearly understood each and every word. Maybe she did understand; who can judge what birds—especially ravens—are capable of knowing? She must have known that she was loved.

Within days she had learned to shout a series of loud *GRAAKs* down the chimney of the fireplace to announce the first light of day, never a popular hour with Stel. When fed, she would fly with her food and cache it in one of a dozen-or-more places. Soon there were caches of mice and chicken and leftover dog food from the neighbors' kennels.

Chickie found she could fly through the open windows of my parked car to explore for treasure, and carried off loose change, business papers, combs, brochures, operating manuals, maps and parking tickets. I once had to fetch my car keys from her cache of shiny stuff, which she kept separate from her food in the bowl of a huge narrow-leafed willow next to the house. It contained bits of foil, coins, a small metal Spitfire, half-a-dozen cinnamon Red Hots and a skull ring from a gumball machine.

I began making a point of rolling up my car windows. Even this did not dissuade her, however; she would zip through the opening as soon as the car door cracked ajar, then fight with her very powerful bill and flicking wings any attempt at ejection. Rather than try to get her out, Stel decided one evening to simply make her run to the convenience store with the raven in the car, which seemed to delight Chickie. She rode with her head out of the sunroof, wings spread for balance, beak open, and tongue lolling, like a happy car dog. Not only that, she discovered the children's cherry cola Slurpees were a delight beyond divine and dipped and gargled the chilly stuff right along with Matt and Cory. Whenever she heard the sliding door of the house, she would head for the car, letting us know she was ready to come along, and assume her exalted position on the top of the backrest.

As the raven moulted in all her new feathers and became fully flighted, we became even more tolerant of Chickie's foibles and were willing victims of her mischievous behavior. Interestingly the Greeks describe errant children with the word *karakaxsa*, a derivative word for the corvid family, which includes ravens.

The neighbors, however, were not so amused. Opening the mail one day, I found an angry note from Mrs. Johnson: our bird was "staining" her lawn furniture. Furthermore the bird was harassing her German shepherds, which I presumed from the note had caused them such stress that they could no longer shepherd Germans and were now in counseling. The note in essence said *control your bird*. Now no bird was truly "ours," especially a raven at hack. The bird belonged to itself in spite of eons of human belief in the ability to control nature.

Could we keep Chickie in the house? Fat chance, as she had already wreaked havoc with a very tough, spiny cactus when she had gotten into the house for less than five minutes. Dinner with Chickie at the table would become not unlike those prison-riot meals in movies, and the pages of precious books would be scattered like leaves amidst the rubble of statuary, audio cassettes and potting soil. (Maybe I am saying "better Mrs. Johnson than us"?)

I had a little talk with the bird. Be reasonable, I suggested, and you can spend your life here in the woods, driving to the 7-Eleven, eating fattening foods, being loved, and preening my hair as you are right now. I explained to Chickie that Mrs. Johnson had sent out letters the year before informing the neighborhood she had hired some boys to shoot magpies that were "pecking" at her German shepherd puppies. I had warned Mrs. Johnson that the discharge of guns was against the county ordinance, and the confrontation had generated longstanding tensions, now directed at Chickie.

The raven blithely ignored my counsel (she was still too young), and promptly tore the screen off one of the doors so she could come in the house while we had dinner. I was dipping an artichoke leaf in hollandaise when lo! she flew to the edge of the table and cocked her head before taking an entire chicken leg off a serving platter. And the very next day I looked out to see her sitting sleepily on Stel's fanny as my wife sunned on the patio.

Came then another note from Mrs. Johnson: *Your bird has pulled all the buttons off my chaise lounge and lawn chair. The bill is enclosed. I am going to shoot that bird.* Enough. I settled with Mrs. Johnson, and we made plans to take Chickie to Bear River Bay Migratory Bird Refuge and release her miles from humans.

On Saturday we drove the seventy-five miles north to Bear River Bay, one of America's first and largest migratory bird refuges with some sixty thousand acres of open wetlands. It had a small resident population of ravens. The boys were crying as we let Chickie out of the car, closed the doors, and drove back to Salt Lake. Hell, we were all crying, concerned she might be shot during the next autumn duck and pheasant hunts, since she might seek out human companionship. Our hope was that she would fly wild and become accustomed and happy to living without humans.

Mrs. Johnson, I might add, was the recipient of karmic come round: she allowed her shepherds to run loose, and on Christmas day, one of the unfortunate animals was shotgunned by an angry neighbor when he caught the dog chasing his horses. The dog was seriously injured but survived, and there was a lengthy investigation by the Humane Society and the Sheriff's Department, all of which resulted in the incident long after referred to by neighbors as The Great Christmas Day Dog Shoot. We were prime suspects, as the shot dog had unfortunately not begun to bleed until he had passed exactly in front of our house. Finally the investigator found blood drops farther up the lane, near the horse-owner's corral. The actual shooter denied it, and our relationship with Mrs. Johnson reached a new low. It's a shame how innocent domestic animals often pay the price of their owners letting them roam freely, and I sensed that Christmas day that something similar could have happened to our beloved raven. We hoped Chiquita was safe and happy.

Diet is everything for birds of prey. Here Steve Chindgren's Kalikak, a hybrid peregrine-prairie falcon, feeds on a pheasant caught in the wild. (Photo by Ray O. Kirkland)

9
FINDING FOOD

I'm truly sorry man's dominion
Has broken nature's social union . . .
—ROBERT BURNS

What are you feeding?" was the single, booming question Stellanie heard when she was introduced as a guest at a meeting of the Rocky Mountain Peregrine Recovery Team, then in the genesis of its reintroduction of the *anatum* species of peregrine falcon to the West. The man with the resonating voice: Morlan Nelson of Boise, thick chested, tan, possessed of ice blue eyes, youthful looking—the Chuck Yeager of raptors, catalyst for much of the academic and applied work on birds of prey during the last forty years in North America.

This one question is enough to tell a raptor expert whether he is talking to a tyro or a pro, since in the keeping of birds of prey, diet is *everything*, avows Jim Enderson, a professor at Colorado College, a Recovery Team member and one of the first, if not the first person, to breed peregrines in captivity.

Stellanie—in awe of this august body of biologists and falconers—gulped her heart back into her chest and answered: "Chicken necks, thighs and legs, mostly. They are darker and have more nutritive value," she added quietly.

"Good!" thundered Nelson. Chicken was a good all-around diet for all birds of prey. Beef had been relegated by us to emergency-ration status, as beef-fed raptors eventually sicken and die over the long run. Ideally coturnix quail or rodents were desirable, but were in short supply and expensive when they could be found.

We were regularly prowling supermarkets for chicken bargains, and we doctored the chicken as we had originally done with beef: adding bonemeal, ABDEC vitamins and sometimes casting material. At first we fed bits directly from the hand, and continued to do so with baby birds. With adults we placed a portion of food in each box or at the base of the perch, then moved on, the bird having the good sense to feed itself. Sometimes a bird would have to be coaxed to eat by opening a mouse and exposing the red flesh, or by rubbing its feet with a bit of chicken.

All raptors, including corvids, cast up small pellets of undigested parts of their diet, and there are two schools of thought on castings: One says they are essential since that is exactly what the bird does in the wild. The other says that birds under many circumstances have been fed on a soft diet without casting material, and the birds have been fine for twenty-or-more years in captivity. "Natural seemed right" to us, so we regularly fed feathers and fur so each bird could occasionally cast.

To give an idea of the quantity of food needed, an eagle will eat about a pound of chicken a day, a red-tail will consume five-to-six ounces, and a kestrel will eat an ounce to an ounce and a half. In the winter every bird metabolizes faster and eats 10 to 15 percent more. We had up to sixty birds on any given day now, requiring a minimum of fifteen-to-thirty pounds of chicken, depending on the mix of large and small raptors.

I bought chicken necks in bulk from a poultry wholesaler, but they were not always available. Frank, our local butcher, saved chicken necks and backs until he had enough to make it worth our while, and often called when he had specials on chicken. When such bulk plenitude became available, we stuffed it in a bulging freezer given us by the USF&WS, as chicken turns bad in a very short time. This meant that meal planning for the birds had to take place several hours in advance of the actual feeding, in order to have the meat thawed and edible. Sometimes Stel rapidly thawed a chicken part by wrapping it in a plastic bag and dropping it in warm water. She always tried to give the birds their food at as close a temperature to live prey as possible.

We let a few falconers and conservation officers know we needed food, and the word passed like lightning. Once we began making our needs known, kind people everywhere called offering food for the birds.

A local pigeon fancier offered his culls. We took some of them, freezing them after slaughter to terminate all possibility of frounce or trichomoniasis, a killing condition commonly shared by raptors and pigeons. On the plus side, pigeon is the richest of all flesh and is preferred by falconers in the feeding and training of birds of prey, and the hawks show a preference for it. These pigeons were rich and fat, but filled the house with feathers since the hawk or owl plumed them, creating cleaning problems that already had Stel too busy. Additionally feathers floating into the intake on the furnace combusted, releasing a nauseating aroma throughout the house. Eventually we quit feeding pigeons when Stel learned they were carrying *Falco herpesvirus*.

A call came one evening from a lady working in the artificial heart laboratory at the University of Utah, announcing they were delivering a whole sheep to us the next morning. Thunderstruck, Stellanie simply thanked them, just as she had done with a Taylorsville lady who had given us a cut-up, frozen goat. Our raptors could not have a diet of this kind of food, but some zoo animals could, so we gave these animals to Hogle Zoo and thanked these thoughtful people for their gifts.

A shy conservation officer brought us the head and neck of a whistling or tundra swan, legal game in Utah, which made a fine meal for an eagle. To meet the challenge of a USF&WS gift of confiscated mallards and pintail ducks, Al Heggen made ready to clear out the evidence freezer at the UDWR, which overjoyed us with the prospect of an unending supply of confiscated game.

The elation was short-lived. Scotty Nichols, a falconer friend and neighbor, called to tell us his prairie falcon was losing weight rapidly, had no appetite and was very weak. Stel diagnosed the problem as lead poisoning, and an X ray by Scott's father, an M.D., confirmed her suspicion: a single lead shotgun pellet had been ingested by Scott's bird when he had been fed a duck they had killed. The falcon died within a few days, and we decided that we could no longer feed "gift" game that had been shotgun killed, only that which we knew was pellet clean and free from disease. It made me wonder what kind of secondary mortality rates existed for raptors feeding on lead-shot ducks and other game left in the field.

"Now this has gone too far," I sputtered one day as I pulled into the driveway and looked at what I was certain was another "gift" of raptor food: it was a whole, dead, two-hundred-pound emu, stuffed into the back of a Volkswagen Rabbit, its giant legs folded neatly against the back window. I could see myself parceling this bird into single servings. I was mightily relieved when it turned out that Julie Lee, a friend, had stopped by to visit while taking the carcass of the emu, which had died at Tracy Aviary after eating some weirdness thrown to it by the unthinking public, to Brigham Young University, home of Clayton White's taxonomy laboratory. The carcass was for scientific study, not for food. I often like to think of Julie driving the fifty miles down the busy interstate with that emu.

"Can you use a few rabbits?" the caller asked. Stel said yes, if they were freshly killed and contained no lead or other toxins.

"How many do you have?" asked Stel.

"Just a dozen" was the answer.

Okay. A dozen bunnies, each cut into three half-pound bunny bites. It sounded reasonably easy to handle—until we saw them. These dozen rabbits looked huge to me—more like horses. Each weighed twenty pounds, and they were freshly slaughtered and still bleeding in four cardboard boxes. I would be forever butchering them!

"Not so fast," said Stel brightly as she hung up the phone. She had been talking to a friend who was also working with raptors. They had a scheme. The rabbits went whole into the freezer, which fortunately was at its capacity nadir. Two days later, when they were solid blocks of icy meat and bone, our friend's husband buzzed them into portion-sized servings with his band saw (that's what a college degree in engineering is all about). We slipped each portion into a plastic storage bag, which could then be thawed as needed. The birds loved it, and it was no longer surprising to see how rapidly two hundred pounds of meat disappeared, especially with our increasing eagle load.

With brilliance born of too much wine, I concluded baby chicks would be good food, and purchased a hundred of them for a few dollars, thinking to freeze them and feed them one at a time. First problem: dispatching a hundred chicks, made difficult as soon as Cory named the first one George. Second problem: tears of outrage and anger as each chick was killed. Third problem: the horrid feeling of knocking tiny chicks senseless, one by one, the fluffy bodies warm in my hand.

Luckily Stel's research brought into question the nutritive value of chicks, especially the lack of calcium, which seems to be almost nil in chicks less than six weeks of age. We quit buying chicks.

Our friend Roger from the aviary called: would we be interested in buying on a regular basis the prepared carnivore food the aviary fed its birds of prey? It sounded good. Stel did a bit of research on the product, described to us as basically beef—the whole cow was put through a grinder, bones and all. No doubt it was good for maintaining many carnivores, but calls to our falconer friends and others indicated that no bird fed on a steady diet of this mix had been known to breed. Well, we had birds that needed to heal, and they needed the best diets we could provide. We tried this beef mixture for a few less-critical birds. It was very soft, and hard for the birds to eat, so we quit feeding it within days. Roger said they supplemented the stuff with whole mice, when they could get them.

Whole mice are like gold. We fed them from time to time, especially to problem patients like Cheech owl when he was paralyzed. The birds took to mice instantly, and got fat on them. Additionally our birds always exhibited good feather condition when on mice. Research on birds of prey held in captivity shows decreases in vital body chemicals and glandular function if they do not regularly kill fresh food, so often I haunted the pet shops to find live mice to feed. Finding them was difficult, although a few stores carried mice as "feeders" for snakes, which need a mouse once a month. A kestrel needs one mouse a day, a red-tail five or six, an eagle sixteen to eighteen. At fifty cents a mouse,

I was facing a second mortgage in order to finance the hawk food.

We strived for nontoxic food, but once we were fooled with disastrous results. In our never-ending search for rodents, Stellanie had called a number of research laboratories asking for any culls they might have. She specifically said they had to be totally free of any chemicals since they were to be used to feed raptors, and raptors were extremely sensitive etcetera.

As a result we soon received a visit from a man who brought us twenty-five rats, at one dollar each, and fifty mice, at fifty cents each, and since we were desperate, we paid him what he asked. His name was Bowman; he was round, had no chin, and possessed porcine eyes that were emotionless. He made me feel as if he were always looking over his shoulder, and was somewhat evasive about how the rats and mice were used at the laboratory, where he worked as a minor functionary. He had me make a check to him personally, and asked to see my check-protection card. After he left, I speculated to Stel that he might be getting his rodents without the knowledge of his bosses, as he seemed uncomfortable.

Bowman showed up several more times with mice and rats and when in need, we purchased them. One morning he called Stel and said he had a batch of rats and mice that were fresh killed, and that they had been experimented on, but he assured her again and again when she pressed him that they were clean of any chemicals. "They have incisions where they did something to them," he said, "but I guarantee that these are good rats and mice."

Desperate, Stel took the rats and mice. Each had a neat slice in its stomach cavity.

The birds fed eagerly on the rodents, and less than an hour later, I got a call from a very concerned Stel. "Muscles is looking low," she said, "and I'm worried. I'm going to watch her."

Twenty minutes later I got another call, and this time Stel had anguish in her voice. "Not only Muscles, but Strider and Pepita are looking very strange. They just sit without any ... animation," she said. The smaller birds were all looking sleepier by the minute. Even a rough-leg was "goofy," she said.

Another call, fifteen minutes later. The concern and anguish had turned to anger: "That son-of-a-bitch Bowman has given us rodents with *something* in them! These birds are all drugged and falling down, whether they're standing on the ground or on the floor. I'm calling that bastard right now," she raged, clicking off.

Bowman at first denied there was anything in the rodents, trying to placate my angry wife. She would have none of it. "I want to know what is in those mice and rats and I want answers in fifteen minutes," she said. I know the voice she used, and it would chill the devil.

Bowman taunted her, a big mistake.

"Either get me the answers or you'll answer to the U.S. Fish and Wildlife Service for killing federally protected birds. We'll have a lab analysis of these mice and rats done. But before I do any of that, I'll call your bosses and tell them what you've been up to," she said, the last comment a bluff but one that apparently hit its mark.

Five minutes later her phone rang. The rats and mice had been injected with cannabinol and phenobarbital compounds, and their organs had been removed for examination.

Our birds were stoned, which might have ended humorously, except one of the kestrels died the next day, and a number of other birds did not fully recover for five days.

"Is this the Audubon?" said a very cockney accent on the telephone. No, we weren't the Audubon Society, but we did take care of birds.

"I 'ear ye need mice?" Yes indeed, mice were nice.

"Me name's Bert Robson and I'm at the Vivarium, the rodent colony for the University of Utah Medical School and University Hospital."

Bert Robson was about to become one of the most important persons in our lives. Referred by a friend, Bert gave all the excess mice bred in the rodent colony to us for the next several years. By now "we" were an organization called the Utah Raptor Group, and eventually we became the Raptor Society, but Bert forever insisted on calling us "the Audubon."

I drove to the Vivarium the next day, finding the rodent colony in the warm basement of an old World War II barracks near the hospital. The dank, warm, unmistakable odor of rodents mixed with wood shavings offended my nostrils, and I tried to hold my breath at first. Finding that impossible, I discovered that after a few minutes I had become inured to the fragrance, and finally located Bert in the basement: a short, slender, mustachioed man with graying hair and a resolute face. He moved quickly to a grouping of about twenty-five rodent trays—plastic tubs with indented wire tops, each affixed with a water bottle and spigot and some still with rodent food pellets. They sat on a table and were marked with a handwritten note: "for the Audubon."

Bert had lived most of his life in Great Britain ("I was an antiaircraft gooner durin' the war," he disclosed to me one day). Bert's charges were the thousands of mice and rats the lab purchased, raised, and issued to the various University of Utah departments, and Bert took a personal view of the creatures. He found them interesting "in their way," he said. It is not as easy to keep rodents as I had thought, and in spite of the fragrance, the rodent colony was spotless, its painted floors and walls washed and disinfected regularly, its ventilating, air-conditioning and heating system providing specially filtered air to help prevent disease or illness.

Mice and rats bred to specific guidelines cost up to a hundred dollars each for individual rodents where purity of genetic strain must be absolutely guaranteed. These and others like them are raised in large colonies in Maine and California, then shipped to research labs and universities across the country. Mice with names like "Swiss-Webster" and "B47s" arrive at the labs and are used in everything from psychology experiments to cancer research. They are well cared for, yet I came to understand how animal-rights people might oppose animal experimentation. These were warm, curious creatures, each with its own life dignity.

Some rodents that arrive at the Vivarium (the department was called Vivarial Sciences) are placed in breeding colonies to provide less expensive animals for experimentation. Since there are frequent population explosions within the colony, Bert was able to provide us with three hundred mice the first day.

I had had no idea there would be that many. My plan had been to simply rap each mouse against a hard surface and put them into plastic bags of four or five each. I reached into a tray, took the first mouse by the tail and swung him in a loop against the surface of the table.

"Please . . . don't do that here," Bert said with gentle, pleading eyes. I was beginning to understand. Any life can be important, and it is made all-the-more so by your familiarity with it. I had my usual problem: how to dispatch a large gift of live food, including some very young, pink babies curled in the bottom of the shavings, or "floof," as Bert called it. I hated this part of the hawk business. Bert produced several wood-and-screen shipping boxes to carry the mice home in. Their hot little bodies steamed the inside windows of the car and filled it with a pungent mouse-shit odor that permeated everything and lingered, to reappear even days later after the car had been in the sun on a warm afternoon.

At home I took each small, sniffing white mouse and dispatched it with a sharp swing against the concrete deck. A number were kept alive for immediate feeding. As I swung mice, I looked up to see the boys watching me with round eyes. Cory had his trumpet in his hand, and Matt was grubby from his latest mine tunnel into the hillside below the house.

"Help, please? If we all do this, we can share the guilt," I said. After a minute Cory put down his horn, Matt took off his miner's hard hat, and the three of us swung mice. Then we bagged them and placed them in the freezer where their hot bodies began melting the ice.

All the house birds received at least one dead mouse. Pepita promptly ate the head of his and stashed the rest in a cache in the headboard of our bed near the berserk clock radio, a fact unknown to me until late in the evening when I attempted to set the radio without first looking.

Bert called again. Another load of mice was available, and one of the conservation officers had suggested that we might get a garbage can with a tight-fitting lid and simply fill it with water and drown them. "G'idea," as Matt always said, and worth trying.

This turned out to be more traumatic than bonking them. I lifted the lid after several minutes to find a mass of swimming mice, their noses held high, climbing furiously on one another as they treaded mice and water. It looked like a cauldron boiling with pink and white valentine candies. This simply would not do. Use auto exhaust? No, there would be lead and other toxins concentrated in the mouse carcasses, to be passed on to the birds.

The aforementioned conservation officer now came up with another idea, one that I am reluctant to relate, but in the interest of science and the prevention of our experience ever happening to another raptor worker, here it is (it *seemed* so right at the time): C.O.s always carry a powerful, stubby firecracker with a side fuse called an M-80, useful for frightening deer and elk from the fields of farmers who often call the UDWR for assistance in protecting their crops. Our C.O. proposed that we place the mice in our trash can; then he would drop a lighted firecracker in the can and we would clamp the lid on. We theorized that the concussion would dispatch all of the mice instantly.

Mice in can, sizzling firecracker in can, lid on can: *WHOOM!* The lid sailed skyward thirty feet, followed by a tumbling column of pink and white mice that rose even higher, some of them sailing in slow motion into the leaves of the narrow-leafed willow far above. We found only a single dead mouse in the can, and none on the ground, and had to cover our heads to protect ourselves from the rain of live, but probably deaf, rodents. I was emotionally somewhere between disgust and hysteria.

In desperation I called a falconer friend who was familiar with the coturnix quail colonies used to breed food for the Peregrine Fund, then located in Fort Collins, Colorado. "How do they kill their quail?" I asked, knowing they must put down several hundred or even a thousand at a time, for they had a large operation. He told me they used a chamber filled with dry ice. The carbon dioxide displaced the oxygen, and the quail expired painlessly and quickly.

When the next load of mice was offered, I stopped at our local ice company and bought the minimum order of five pounds of dry ice. I placed it in the bottom of the battered can, now bulging but still airtight. Over this I put a layer of newspaper. I then placed the mice on top of the newspaper and closed the lid.

Five minutes later I knew I had found the solution to my grisly problem, but it still was never an easy task. I was hating this ending of life more and more, even knowing that these deaths gave life to creatures I loved. I was beginning to think in life-and-death cycles and to understand that in order for anything to live, something must die—whether it be food for hawks or for humans.

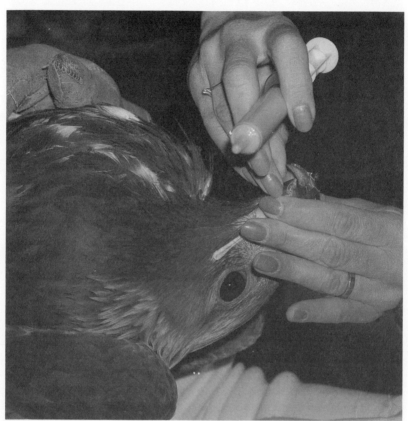

Stellanie prepares to gavage an injured golden eagle with a mixture designed to hydrate and nourish the bird. (Photo by Marie R. Kirkland)

10

HOLDING BIRDS:
TRIAGE AND TREATMENT

> *. . . Among the thorns and*
> *dangers of this world.*
>
> —SHAKESPEARE

Once sheltered and nourished, our hawks became the subjects of an investigation to determine why they had come to us, what troubled them, and how long they would stay.

Sometimes a conservation officer would bring a confiscated bird in obvious good health. Stellanie would handle the bird only long enough to see if it was fat; then the bird was placed in a box for a temporary hold until chamber space or perch space became available for it. Sometimes these birds could be released immediately, but more often they had to be held until a court had made a determination of their case—and that could mean several months of care from us.

Often a bird came just looking low, its head down, perhaps unable to rise. Stel would palpate to check it for broken bones and general condition, look in its mouth, perhaps observe it in the house in a box for several hours or days.

Birds obviously shot up or otherwise suffering from trauma arrived frequently, covered with blood, bones protruding, in shock, beaks open, tongues arched, hissing like serpents or crying in pain. These birds needed immediate medical treatment and intensive care.

All birds suspected of having any health problems, including dehydration or prolonged periods without food, were administered a healthy dose of Stellanie's Gatorade-Nutri-Cal-vitamin solution as a matter of course. Only the obviously healthy (usually we knew their origins) escaped this treatment, and virtually all birds were fed immediately upon arrival, although some refused to eat.

Young birds arrived in batches in the spring, sometimes still in nests from the felled trees they had occupied, with a nearly tearful, burly construction worker gently carrying them. Birds came in boxes, in cages, or flying loose inside automobiles.

On a single day in June, we received three Swainson's hawks and two red-tails, all at a stage falconers call branchers. In a production line, we jessed them, attached leashes, then staked them out in the creek bottoms on block perches after giving each a shot of Stel's mixture. A little later I went to the bottoms and tried each of them on a bit of chicken, which they ignored. The next morning each responded voraciously to a white mouse, and thereafter they would bate in unison at anyone approaching their area, a lesson in how quickly young birds imprint, and how the behavior of the group may accelerate the process through continuous reaffirmation. We had been warned to beware of these young, semitame birds, as they occasionally go for the human face when instant gratification in the way of food is not forthcoming. We were all cautious, but later complacency proved painful for Stel, as we shall see.

As these young red-tails and Swainies (as we called them) were awaiting court decisions, we received a lovely young male kestrel, neatly jessed—with his beak cut back. Apparently his holder had decided to clip the sharp, down-curved portion of the beak, and had cut it back so the bird looked like one of my tumbler pigeons. Because he was unable to tear any food, the kestrel was skinny, and we had to feed him small bits of chicken, which required additional preparation. Soon the bird's beak began showing signs of regrowth, and within two months we were able to release him, whole, healthy, and rapacious looking. In another case a prairie falcon with a split beak was repaired by a friend using Super Glue. The bond held until the beak could naturally fuse.

Some birds were not injured, yet needed intensive attention, especially accipiters, an example being a young Cooper's hawk that arrived one rainy spring evening. We called him Shuper, for reasons of sibilance, I suppose, and he had to be fed chicken constantly due to the need of accipiters for lots of sugar to maintain their high metabolic rate. Every hour or two he received a full crop of chicken, and just as rapidly he "put over" each meal and was ready to eat again. Shuper grew rapidly: one evening a couple of weeks after he had come to us, we had dinner with friends, Howard and Wilma Marcus, during which the bird had to be fed. I was showing them the hawk, which promptly jumped out of his box and trotted the length of the dining table, leaving his footprints in the butter. I could never again coax Wilma to come for dinner, and eventually Shuper was released in a cottonwood grove near Heber City.

Of all the young birds we got, batches of kestrels were the most delightfully anticipated. They are such jolly, happy little birds, so elegantly marked, so loving when properly cared for. They came in batches of three, four or five, or less frequently as a single youngster. The babies in each nest group would vary in size, the first hatched being the largest, and so on down. At first all huddle in the corner of the box as we look down on them, probably anticipating an awful end at the hands of the round-headed ghouls blocking the light. A tiny bit of chicken is held before the beak of the largest bird, perhaps even rubbed across her feet. Still she holds back, bracing herself mightily into her fellow nestlings as they jam, terrified, into the back of the box. A little chicken across the nares. The moisture left on her beak by the chicken elicits a tongue, a taste. The bird opens her beak slightly. Pop, in goes a morsel, and the surprised bird's little beak opens and closes rapidly as she gulps down the tidbit. Another bit of chicken. Then another. The little kestrel is still braced hard against the back of the box. Then a morsel to a nestmate, then another. Within minutes all are eating hungrily, though still fearful and tense with backs straining.

At the second feeding two or three hours later, the babies are still tense, but they eat hungrily now. By the third feeding, they begin to chirr—*eee*—*eee*—*eee*—*eee*—as they jockey for the best positions to receive the food from above. By the fifth feeding, they begin their feeding chirr whenever a shadow passes before the box's light. Just before feeding, Stel warms the chicken in a plastic bag in hot water; then she adds baby vitamins, and bonemeal, and feeds each batch by hand. If mice are the day's food, they must be shredded and cut in bits so little ones can handle them. Once kestrels have their feathers, a small, whole mouse may be fed, after first having been incised to expose red flesh and also to allow young beaks a purchase on their prey.

As the baby down flakes off, the youngsters begin flapping in anticipation of their first flight. Open a bouncing, shaking box of four-week-old kestrels and you get a face full of billowing, powdery pennae and an earful of gleeful, anticipatory caterwauling.

When I awake at 3:00 A.M., the wind moans in the leaves and branches clatter together, presaging an early-morning thunder-shower. I look toward my closet and see, glowing like a dim Christmas tree light, the control switch of the ever-present heating pad resting beneath the box of sleeping baby kestrels.

From the kitchen I hear the swivel of Tufter's jesses as the great horned owl flies back up to his ring perch, restlessly passing the night. Thank goodness diurnal birds do not feed their young at night; we deem it all right to feed just before we turn in because there's no other time to do it. In three hours we will be up and feeding again, and there are now fifty-three birds in the house, the mews, and on perches. I drift back to sleep.

When the arriving box revealed larger, adult birds or flighted, immature birds, they were almost always hurt or ill. Even the wiser, adult birds fall victim to many human-created problems. Nothing is quite so sad as a proud eagle or falcon torn and bloody or paralyzed and covered with feces. Yet these were the birds most in need of help.

One of our adult golden eagles was such a bird, delivered on a sloppy autumn night in a soaking burlap bag, found by a UDWR conservation officer near the poisoned carcass of a sheep in Utah's Wasatch Mountains. Clearly the eagle was a secondary victim of toxins directed at coyotes, even though poisons like 1080 and thallium had been long ago banned. Some local sheep ranchers have stockpiled the poisons and still use them in defiance of the law, apparently feeling a superior claim to public lands than public creatures.

I was surprised the eagle was not dead, for both poisons are extremely toxic and can kill in seconds. Perhaps the bird had not eaten much, or possibly the poisons react differently in a bird than in a mammal?

"I'm beginning to turn into a misanthrope," said Stel as she examined the eagle. The bird was very low and would not live through the next day. "Grizzly bears eat sheep and have been known to eat people; therefore grizzly bears must be good," she said acrimoniously as she wiped some awful black fluid from the bird's nostrils.

The mood seemed especially pervasive: within days another golden eagle—a younger bird—was brought in, sitting quietly, head bowed and low, ill or injured from causes unknown. "Found in a field near Tremonton" was the only note on its discovery. At first we suspected it was another poison case; then Stel saw a small, black contusion on one foot. As I held the bird with those massive feet gripped firmly in my hands, Stel carefully examined the bird's wings until she found another small contusion with a black scab. Then she knew: this bird was part of an ongoing problem being studied all over the West, and yet to be fully resolved.

Over time, several hawks and eagles had arrived looking ill but without apparent trauma. As our powers of observation became better, Stel noticed these birds had a small, black contusion on one foot. Inevitably the birds died within a few hours or days of our receiving them. Only after Stel had carefully looked over each bird and found a similar black mark did she solve the mystery: these birds were being electrocuted on power lines. The foot provided one contact, and when the bird took off or landed, a wing would make contact and complete the circuit, allowing a powerful electrical charge to burn through the bird.

Morlan Nelson and his protégé, Pat Benson, a young Ph.D. candidate at Brigham Young University (now an authority on South African raptors), spent thousands of hours researching the power-line problem. For nearly five years Pat drove along the power lines in Utah, Nevada, Idaho, Oregon and Wyoming and learned that certain kinds of poles set in certain places were favorites of raptors. Sometimes he found these "hot" poles by watching coyotes, which had learned to trot the lines and eat the carcasses of hawks, owls and eagles that had been electrocuted. "You could tell which poles were problems by the bones beneath them," Patrick told me.

Meanwhile Nelson was shooting motion-picture footage that showed eagles landing on uncharged power lines of the type causing most of the deaths. It was fascinating, as it made clear the difference in flight abilities between young birds and experienced old birds. If I had ever thought a bird did not actually have to "learn" to fly, these films quickly changed my mind. An adult bird flies crisply, maneuvering smoothly and confidently. A young bird is sloppy and slow, and may land with wings teetering and tippling for balance. It is at this moment that many young birds make contact and are electrocuted. Pat also found that wet weather may contribute to the electrocution problem.

Power lines have some benefit, on the other hand. Eagles, hawks and ravens nest in them, and they provide excellent perches for hunting. Most birders watch power-line pole tops for raptors, from kestrels to eagles, for clearly they find them fine perches. (I marvel at the prairie falcons and rough-legged hawks that perch on those huge steel poles when the temperature is ten below. The circulation in the foot of the bird keeps it warm and flexible always, even when on icy steel. My admiration may have to do with a childhood recollection of placing my own bare finger on a snow-shovel blade at ten below during the horrid winter of 1949.)

The power companies have attempted to retrofit the old and dangerous poles discovered by Benson and others with a device called an "Oo," which is triangular in shape and helps prevent a bird from getting a grip. As one power worker explained, "It sort of gooses the eagle before it can land."

Stellanie obtained postmortems on the first few electrocuted birds. Invariably they had died of heart failure, caused by congestion of the heart, created by many volts of power surging through their bodies.

There are many thousands of miles of U.S. power lines still killing thousands of raptors, and while the power companies are trying to modify old lines and erect new, bird-proof ones, the problem still exists, and some say it is being worked upon at a snail's pace.

Shot birds seemed to predominate in autumn and winter, a time coinciding with the hunting seasons in the West. Kestrels often came in during the September dove season, and marsh hawks, short-eared owls and prairie falcons came in during the duck and pheasant seasons of October through December. About November 30, the rough-legged hawks, docile, trusting tundra dwellers unfamiliar with human violence, started falling. With the end of the upland bird and waterfowl seasons, many western hunters pursue black-tailed jackrabbits in the sage deserts, sometimes with high-powered rifles, so January through March brought fewer shotgun injuries, but more victims shot by .22-caliber rifles, or birds shot half away by heavier calibers.

Having always been a hunter, I am sickened by this wanton, senseless blowing away of life, yet clearly remember my own youth of wildlife vandalism. Can these attitudes be changed? I also remember a 1975 study for the USF&WS by Stephen Kellert of Yale on hunters: 85 percent of those he surveyed said they would break the wildlife laws if they thought they could get away with it. And these were waterfowl hunters, the supposed elite of all hunting types. Maybe Stephen Jay Gould is right: maybe humanity is a self-destructive aberration, a greedy mutation, a materialistic mistake.

I would like to think humans can share the earth with other creatures, but a goshawk that came to us sent my estimation of the human race plummeting. Goshawks are dashing, intrepid hunters wearing slate and pinstripes, set off by a brilliant ruby eye. Un-daunted by the presence of humans, goshawks are owl-like in their berserk persistence when hunting prey. As an example, Dr. William Wood of East Windsor Hill, Connecticut, wrote fifty years ago of a goshawk that followed a hen into a house and seized her on the kitchen floor in the presence of a man and his daughter. In Maine a goshawk chased an escaping hen under a woman's skirts. Both hawks were killed, and they have always been an object of hatred by poultrymen and those who have not yet accepted the role of the predator in the natural world.

Our goshawk, brought to us by a falconer, had been found near Draper, Utah, near one of the poultry "factories" of that area. This bird was a big, immature female, still yellow of eye, and handsome in clove brown and cinnamon tans. Her long barred tail, or train, was in perfect condition. Stel examined the bird carefully and found at least two places where blood was caked on her feathers. A closer look indicated puncture wounds from shotgun pellets.

I found a long box in which she could rest comfortably on her stomach and breast. Her legs dangled uselessly, and she was unable to stand, indicating some sort of spinal injury. Stel gavaged the bird with her first-aid mixture to hydrate her and provide nutrients. We put the bird in the box and placed the box in the dining area of the house.

As with so many birds, we could only wait to see if she improved. Sometimes a bird came in with a paralysis that cleared up after a few days; sometimes a bird knocked senseless and apparently dying came around, having suffered only a concussion from flying into a window (and it's very unnerving, I might add, when a bird you think is dead suddenly comes to and starts weaving around the kitchen counter).

This handsome goshawk lay on her stomach all day the first day; that night, still paralyzed in the legs and lower body, she began attempting to flap her wings in the box. *Ka-bump, ka-bump, ka-bump, ka-bump:* on it went, first intermittently, then steadily, as the bird sought to fly from captivity and paralysis.

I moved the box into the furnace room where I thought the noise would be blocked from my ears, but I could still hear it: an endless, reverberating accusation of my species. I remembered all too clearly the birds I had killed; I felt ill. I thought of a passage from Nicholas Monsarrat's *The Cruel Sea*, in which he wished dead a badly injured seaman, and ashamedly I felt the same way about this goshawk.

I wanted to find the poultryman who had shot the bird and ask: "Would it not be simple to screen over your poultry runs?"

I wanted to show this paralyzed hawk to that poultryman's children, just as my own children saw it. Show them a mute-stained and smeared tail, because the bird could no longer stand to defecate. I wanted that poultryman to hear the cries of the bird when I had to lift it so Stel could examine it. The goshawk made sounds of pain and fear, unmistakable sounds from any creature, animal or human.

Three days we waited. Each day the bird lived in pain, slowly slipping. Stel vowed to euthanize her, but the next morning she lay dead in the box bottom, wings slightly spread, head turned on its side, yellow eye open, the feathers of her long tail soiled by her own feces.

Many gun-shot birds made it, in spite of horrendous injuries; strange this one that didn't make it is so unforgettable, like blood in a baby crib.

Some birds were just plain sick, without apparent injury. If their mutes were not a nice healthy white with a splash of green, it indicated possible internal injuries, or possible consumption of poisons. With all the human-created problems, we sometimes lost sight of the fact that there are also common diseases in wild birds.

For these kinds of diagnoses, we had to turn to two doctors who researched such matters at Intermountain Labs, Larry McGill and Jack Taylor. Stellanie would draw blood and deliver it to the doctors, who would then return it with a lab report—and a bill for fifty dollars.

As these reports accumulated, Stel saw a certain pattern in which darker-colored birds of some species seemed more often to have a leucocytozoan condition, a fact which interested these biologists. Soon the three of them had a research project cooked up to study leucocytozoans, resulting in our blood workups being done at no charge. As Drs. McGill and Taylor became more caught up by Stellanie's questions, they often volunteered to do postmortems on dead birds, which resulted in a good deal of medical data which Stellanie was able to share. As word of this trickled into the raptor world, we began getting calls from as far away as England asking Stellanie for medical advice on sick birds of prey, since so much medical information on birds was lacking then.

There are very few diseases human beings can get from birds, but as luck would have it, the Great Hawk saw fit to reward Stellanie with an ugly bout of aspergillosis, which spun her into fits of coughing and agonizing chest pains for several weeks. Her experience with "asper," as it is called, enabled her to help a fellow-raptor worker, Ron Joseph, now with the USF&WS in Maine. Ron had been feeling lousy for weeks and in a phone conversation described his symptoms, which Stellanie recognized immediately. Ron had been handling bald eagles and had picked up asper from one of them. Doctors had been mystified but with the new diagnosis, he was treated properly and soon recovered.

To this day Stellanie carries a thumb-sized scar on one lung from her bout with aspergillosis.

A male bald eagle came to us just after Thanksgiving, not too big, but a perfect caricature of eagleness: ivory head and tail, dark brown wings and body, butter yellow feet and beak. He had a pearl eye with an onyx center, which was not at all subtle, resigned and spiritual like those of our golden eagles, but hard-edged and twitching with indignation.

Stel cast him in a towel and carefully felt her way along his bones and body, finding nothing broken or otherwise out of place. The C.O. who had brought him could offer no information about the bird's discovery and captivity; "found by the road" was all he could tell us about its origins.

We carried the bird to an empty mews chamber and released him, then sat on the bench in front of the mews to admire his magnificent plumage.

The eagle looked around the mews, getting his bearings, seeming to check out the height, width, perches, bars and water pans. Then he sort of hunkered down in the gravel of the mews bottom and *rolled over on his back!* There he stayed, his head up, looking at me across his chest like a patient in a hospital bed or a man on a luge. No longer was he nervous and excited; he looked relaxed and comfortable, as if he were tubing in a gentle river, with his big, taloned feet in relaxed curls on his tail base.

Stel and I looked at each other and roared with laughter.

For the next five days, he stayed in this position, and each time we looked at him, we could not help but laugh as he lay there on his back, glaring at us as if to say he knew exactly what he was doing. And maybe he did.

After a few more days, he was up on his feet and eating heartily (he gobbled a road-killed gull brought by UDWR in less than three minutes, having gone without food for the five days we had had him. We had both golden and bald eagles refuse food for ten days before finally eating).

The University of Minnesota wanted a bald eagle for some research on diet, and Dr. Gary Duke was sent this bird with the understanding he would be released within a few days. A few weeks later, Gary called to tell us he had X-rayed the bird after its arrival and had found indications of traumatic bruising on the eagle's chest. Perhaps he had flown into a car or a fence. I think that by lying on his back, he relieved the pain and pressure, just as I might do by elevating an injured limb to keep the blood from pounding painfully. The bird eventually was released to the wild.

DODGEVILLE PUBLIC LIBRARY
139 S. Iowa St.
Dodgeville, WI 53533

Flying "at hack." Cory with a kestrel released at home that has come down to see if he carried food. (Photo by Stellanie Ure)

A red-tail spreads her wings to bathe in the spray of Stellanie's hose. (Photo by Jim Ure)

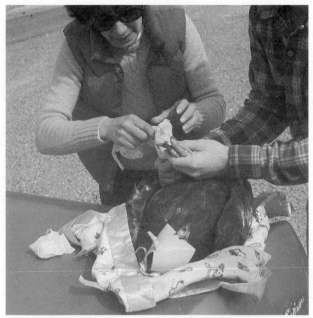

Unwrapping the feet of a golden eagle after transporting for release. (Photo by Jim Ure)

The first mews, finished, painted. (Photo by Stellanie Ure)

Bald eagles rest in the mews prior to release. (Photo by Mike Coffeen)

A young Cooper's hawk warmed by a bedroom lamp. (Photo by Stellanie Ure)

A male prairie falcon sits on the kitchen counter awaiting his mouse dinner. (Photo by Stellanie Ure)

Kestrels get supervised recreation on the sunny lawn. (Photo by Stellanie Ure)

Swainson's hawk launches from a power pole, sometimes a deadly perch for raptors. (Photo by Ray O. Kirkland)

Kestrels on the "hack board," a feeding station for free-flying birds. (Photo by Stellanie Ure)

Scott Nichols's female prairie falcon in its first year. It died after lead poisoning was misdiagnosed. (Photo by Jim Ure)

11

VARIOUS VETS

*And when the physician said, "Sir,
you are an old man," "That happens,"
replied Pausanias, "because you were
never my doctor."*

—PLUTARCH

Falconers are bird-crazed souls, too, and will be found congregating wherever raptors collect. As our collection of various birds in recovery grew, so did our visits by falconers, who offered wit and wisdom, and advice, whether needed or not.

Sometimes falconer advice was in conflict, but there was one fact on which all falconers seemed to agree: there were no skilled bird veterinarians in Utah. There were a few bird vets elsewhere, but the nearest were in Boise, Reno, or Colorado Springs. Even the veterinarians agreed, and those we called to ask about possible treatment of raptors readily admitted their training had largely excluded any information about bird diseases or pathology.

There were good reasons for this, the first being that birds up until then had not enjoyed the popularity as pets that we see today, so there was no demand for veterinary services, and no money to be made from them. (In England, interestingly, veterinarians are supposed to treat wildlife at no charge.) Horses, dogs and cats were all well known to veterinary science, but avian medical knowledge was largely an outgrowth of work being done for commercial poultrymen in the southern states (although the initial discovery of the AIDS virus actually was made in birds in 1913).

And we cannot forget that when reduced to basics, birds are living fossils—very much like the reptilian dinosaurs of the Triassic period, and perhaps vertebrate paleontologists were more knowledgeable about birds in the 1970s than were veterinarians.

Complex, airy bone structures, some of them part of the bird's respiratory system; strange internal organs, including gizzards with rocks in them; high metabolism; reproductive organs that created calcium-shelled ova; feathers that belonged in specific places and had specific functions—why, it was enough to drive a dog-and-cat man nuts. "Well, they *are* warm-blooded," said one vet, scratching his head as he sought to find similarities. We continued to treat the birds ourselves, calling on aviculturists and falconers for knowledge and experience.

The trouble which we and others would take to secure quality veterinary care was illustrated one dark January night when Steve Chindgren, looking funereal and anguished, arrived at our house carrying "BBG," his gyrfalcon; the bird was in deep shock. Steve had come to respect the knowledge of avian physiology and medicine Stellanie had acquired, and was now turning to her for diagnostic and first-aid advice. BBG had been tail-chasing a big rooster pheasant at breakneck speed across a stubble field in Davis County. The wily old rooster had used a barbwire fence to his advantage, slipping through the strands, which BBG struck as she attempted to clutch the pheasant. BBG was spun to the ground where she lay panting, wings akimbo, until Steve had sprinted to her. Her leg hung limply and at a strange angle from her body. Stel checked her over slowly, carefully feeling the leg and hip socket as Steve held his breath.

Stel's verdict: a dislocation of the leg. She could find no broken bones. "You'll have to have the leg reset," she said, and refused to even attempt to do it herself. The bird needed an X ray and an anesthetic in order for the job to be done properly.

Steve had a backlog of unhappy experiences with local veterinarians, so we started making calls to Boise, Colorado Springs, Laramie, and finally, Reno. He discussed with each doctor the bird's problem, and listened carefully as they asked questions and commented.

Finally Steve called Steve Baptiste, a longtime falconer and breeder in Reno. "He cares about birds," Baptiste said of the Reno vet he used, which meant that the man cared enough to listen, and that he had some knowledge of avian medicine. That was enough for Steve.

Steve asked me to join him on the trip and in less than an hour, we were in Steve's VW van freezing our appendages off. Steve and Stellanie had a brief debate over heat and cold for the bird, Steve insisting that the bird, an arctic resident, should be kept cool, while Stel argued that anything in shock needed warmth, and encouraged Steve to place BBG on a heating pad.

Steve's cool-is-best theory prevailed, and it was a chilly five-hundred-mile drive through the star-sparkled Great Basin. Regular doses of tequila seemed to keep my metabolism at blast-furnace levels, and the stuff got me to Reno at dawn with a modicum of comfort. Three hours sleep, the vet at 9:00 A.M.,the procedure completed by 11:00 with the bird's leg in place: by now I was feeling raw and angular. A nap, followed by dinner at a fine French restaurant, fixed me up nicely, and we arrived back in Salt Lake the next night with BBG on her way to recovery. The trip was a fifty-six-hour example of the lengths to which dedicated bird people will go for help for their raptors.

Avian veterinary help did finally come to Salt Lake City a few months later. One morning our beloved canary Barnaby, a veritable Elton John of singing rollers, took ill; he was weak and drooping, with dripping nostrils. In desperation Stellanie called a new vet in town named Phillip Ensley, of whom a falconer had cautiously said "he seemed to really *like* birds," the best endorsement of a local vet we had heard at that time. Ensley showed Stel how to administer antibiotics using a tent over Barnaby's cage, with a vaporizer introducing a mix of drugs in its moist air.

Alas, Barnaby departed this temporal world, but Ensley agreed to have a look at one of our eagles, a bird of "high interest" to state and federal wildlife services. Not only that, he made a house call. The eagle's problems were unknown, except that she looked very sick; her head was down, she evidenced little movement, and her condition was very weak. Ensley said he suspected poisoning.

The eagle was taken from her box and spread on a picnic table outdoors, where a rolled towel was set into the grip of her mighty talons. With great gentleness Ensley swabbed the wing feathers to reveal the collapsed brachial vein in her wing, hard to get at because of the bird's poor circulation; at last the needle found the vein. As Ensley injected glucose into the brachial, the bird gripped the towel more tightly, but otherwise did not struggle or resist; her brown eyes were bright and clear and totally without fear.

Next Ensley took a syringe and a tube of Nutri-Cal from his bag, our introduction to the high-calorie supplement which provides much nutrition in small doses that are both easy to administer and easy for birds to digest. The paste is squeezed from a tube, mixed with water, sucked into a syringe without a needle, then gavaged into the bird's throat. Stellanie was already administering Pedialyte or Gatorade, sometimes hyped with egg yolk and vitamins, as a means of quickly hydrating and nourishing a downed bird. Now Nutri-Cal proved to be a helpful addition to first-aid treatment, and in some cases, long-term care.

As Ensley washed up, he again expressed his opinion that the bird might have been poisoned, and that about all we could do was keep her hydrated and nourished and hope for the best. For the next four days, we force-fed the bird four times a day. She was so sick she seldom resisted when I held her in my arms as Stel gavaged her. On the fifth day she was lying flat in the pen, wings slightly spread, eyes almost shut, breathing slowly and shallowly. Stel warmed an old blanket and placed it over the bird, then sat with her until she died.

The next morning Stel met Auston Johnson, a wiry old-time conservation officer dispatched by the UDWR, who stopped to pick up the eagle carcass (by law it had to be turned over to wildlife agents). Stel, having no experience with Johnson and his well-known black humor, watched as the man pulled on huge rubber gloves that came clear to his elbows. Said Johnson: "I hope you didn't get any thallium poison on you, 'cause if you did, you'll be gone in forty-eight hours."

Stellanie was on the phone to the University of Utah poison-control center in ten seconds flat, and then called me breathlessly to warn that if I started to feel ill, it was just too bad; there wasn't much that could be done about thallium poisoning. While Johnson was having fun at our expense, we nonetheless took more precautions thereafter.

Ensley regularly appeared at our house for several months, providing knowledge and free service after hours, a fortunate turn of events since the UDWR and the USF&WS had no money to spare for veterinary help.

The search for veterinary care in those early days created problems, both ethical and financial. It would have been nice if the professionals we dealt with for services had felt somewhat more altruistic, yet we recognized they had to make money for their skills. Sometimes you simply could not afford to privately pay for the vet (most often payment came out of our pockets), but you did not want to lose the creature which had struggled so valiantly over almost insurmountable odds, and at last you felt as if some higher power were telling you to write that check, regardless of the consequences. Often I agonized and blustered over money; today I have no regrets, in spite of my recollections of rodent, veterinary and laboratory bills totaling eight hundred dollars in a single month. Phil Ensley was a godsend, and others must have known it, for he was hired away by the National Zoo in Washington, D.C., and at last report was practicing avian medicine to his heart's content at the San Diego Zoo.

Alas, the falconers' perceptions about local vets proved accurate for some time after Ensley's departure, and we regularly listened to tales of woe about misdiagnosed, mistreated and mishandled birds.

Stel performed daily treatment, researched on her own, contacted other rehabilitators and vets in places as far away as Minnesota and Texas (the late Shawn Ogburn, a dear friend and one of the ice-breaking rehabilitators), and gave a lot of birds back to the sky, sometimes never knowing what had originally troubled them: time, rest, good food and isolation were great healers for many birds. But she was in need of X-ray services, and only veterinarians had that equipment.

Our second vet, "Dr. Aldrich,"(the names of the guilty veterinarians have been changed) turned out to be a *megalo kephalos* of the first magnitude, knowing all there was to know. Aldrich was reputed to have had experience with reptiles, so we reasoned that bird medicine might come naturally.

One thing Ensley had taught us was that he did not know everything, and that he needed Stellanie's ever-expanding knowledge, which she discreetly and diplomatically disclosed as long as the vet was willing, or bludgeoned him with if he was not, often sending copies of learned medical treatises back to vets to underscore her point.

At first Dr. Aldrich seemed to listen; all she needed was an X ray for now, Stellanie explained. He went along with that, and together they read the film, examining the splintered radius of this particular red-tail. He made some vague suggestions that he should operate and piece it back together. Stellanie applied the first rule of bird healing: wait and see. Sometimes less is more.

A few weeks later we received another golden eagle, its yellow feet covered with ugly brown scabs. "It *looks* like avian pox," Stel said, researching from a book on avian medicine published by the University of Iowa.

"Oh no, not a pox," Dr. Aldrich assured us, examining the eagle the next day. "Dermatitis," and he argued with all kinds of vigor and apparent knowledge that he must remove the skin from the leg. Stel feared it would dry out the muscle tissue. "Oh, we'll keep it wet and packed." Reluctantly we agreed, since he *was* the *vet*.

He peeled the skin and within two days, true to Stel's prediction, the muscle dried and the leg became useless. This meant amputation, and at the time we knew of no eagle breeders who could take an eagle with an amputated leg, since injured eagles tend to breed well in captivity. Neither did we know of any exhibits that needed or would take a one-legged eagle. The bird's leg grew worse, in spite of Dr. Aldrich's smooth talk and boasting. The eagle finally had to be euthanized, and a lab pathology on the bird clearly showed it had avian pox, just as Stel had suspected.

We stopped using Dr. Aldrich's services, but at least one other bird lover came to grief because of the doctor's hubris: first he flatly told our friend there had never been a case of trichomoniasis reported in birds of prey, a disease called frounce first described by Frederick II in his remarkable book on falcons written in the thirteenth century, about which we shall hear more later. Frounce is also called canker in pigeons and is passed to the falcons which eat them. Unforgivably Dr. Aldrich also failed to diagnose as lead poisoning the illness of this friend's prairie falcon, which died after ingesting a single lead pellet, clearly visible in Dr. Aldrich's X ray of the bird's gullet.

Dr. Aldrich now shunned, Stel was back to doing daily diagnosing and treatment on her own, until two birds came to us with dragging, broken wings. One was a red-tail, the other a prairie falcon; both were in good health with no other apparent problems. Sometimes wing injuries heal easily, but they are tricky, especially for falcons which use their wings for intricate aerobatics. But red-tails can "pole hunt" and survive in the wild without perfect wing articulation, being adaptable and less specialized. It's another problem altogether with hawks and falcons that migrate up to eight thousand miles—Swainson's hawks and peregrines go clear to Argentina.

Stel needed X rays on these two birds, and she called a nearby vet, "Dr. Bloomquist." After conversing with him, she felt as if we could take a chance. At least, she reasoned, she would work with him up to the X-ray state of diagnosis, then decide her next steps. The red-tail proved to have a broken ulna.

"Let me pin that," said Dr. Bloomquist. Stel thought about it, then agreed, and the vet proceeded to work a pin into the bird's wing bone. When he completed the surgery, he had wrapped the bird as tightly as King Tut's mummy. "Please don't wrap birds so tightly," Stel said, uncomfortable about telling a medical professional his job.

At home she cut the constricting bandages loose and rewrapped the wing with a proper sling, then placed the bird in a box for recovery. Usually a bone began setting in a bird in four-to-five days. It would be weeks before the bird could go to a holding pen or flight chamber in the mews, where it would get exercise and more observation to determine if it was releasable.

Meanwhile the prairie falcon was now prepared for X ray, and Dr. Bloomquist could clearly see the break in its wing on the film he held up to the overhead light, as the still-wet frame holding the X ray dripped water onto his bald pate. The doctor suggested inserting metal pins into the wing, a surgical procedure that caused Stel some misgivings, what with us not having any track record with this vet. But the UDWR authorized the surgery and agreed to pay the bill, so Stel told the doctor to go ahead. We took the bird home that evening, heavily anesthetized.

Next morning the falcon was awake but far from alert, and she had worked out of her dressing. The vet wanted to see her, but since neither of us could take her back that day, a UDWR worker volunteered to do it. When he returned, he held a dying prairie falcon in his hands, a victim of too much anesthetic and the suffocation of too-tight bandaging that held the wing next to the body in a vicelike grip.

Stel frantically stripped the heavy wrapping away from the bird's constricted body, revealing massive *stainless-steel* sutures in the wing, each carefully tied in bites that sunk into feather, flesh and bone. The doctor, God bless him, was used to treating powerful horses and dogs, not delicate birds.

The crowning blow, however, came with the red-tail: the pin the doctor had placed in its wing worked out of the ulna and traveled clear up the neck of the hawk, where it worked its way out through the skin. I watched Stel pull the long, curved wire out with her hand. Remarkably this red-tail was perfectly flighted and was placed with a falconer, who watched it escape weeks later, bumping ever higher against cumulus clouds as it sailed out of sight.

As a result of this experience, anesthetic tables showing dosages per ounce of bird were thereafter presented to each veterinarian we dealt with.

The next veterinarian was "Dr. Collier," a society vet, well known in the community. By now Stellanie had acquired excellent diagnostic and treatment skills, and Dr. Collier listened carefully and asked the right questions. For a while we felt we had a good combination of home and clinical care, but as Stel reviewed her records a few months after we had begun to work with Collier, certain patterns became clear: when birds got only X rays and consultation at the clinic, followed by home health care, many were released. Yet not a single bird which Dr. C. had operated on and retained for any period of time had been releasable. It was as if the doctor had the knowledge about how to treat the birds, but that in the process of treatment, his fingers somehow did not get the message from his brain.

One day a friend and television newsman joined Stel and the vet as they worked on an eagle. Lights, camera, action:

CAMERA MEDIUM CLOSE-UP OF OPERATING ROOM AND OCCUPANTS

Newsman (voice-over): We're here in the clinic of Dr. Collier where he and Stel Ure, a raptor rehabilitator, are working on a golden eagle.

CAMERA GOES CLOSE UP ON DR. COLLIER WITH X RAY

Newsman: Well, Dr. Collier, how does it look for the bird?

Dr. Collier: This bird will be just fine. It'll fly soon.

Stellanie: Cut. Cut. Oh shit, cut.

CAMERA JIGGLES. SCREEN GOES BLACK

It was at this juncture that Stel maneuvered the doctor into the next room, away from the news crew. She pointed out what the doctor had failed to see on the X ray—and had missed when he had examined the bird—that its entire wingtip was missing, shot cleanly away. He was concentrating on a secondary shot break, showing that even skilled vets sometimes fail to look at the whole bird. His care was not wrong, but it was not right enough.

And then the Great Hawk smiled down and our veterinary luck turned. I entered my living room one evening to see sitting, military straight, looking slightly uncomfortable, a tall, slender, movie-star-handsome man with steel blue eyes and dark hair. He was talking to Stel, I was instantly jealous, and he was Dr. Greg Ivins, then interning in human medicine at the University of Missouri Medical Center in Columbia.

Greg had been a falconer since childhood, and had worked with a veterinarian as a volunteer since he was twelve years old. He and Stel had met over the phone after a newspaper clipping on her work had been sent to him. On a trip to the University of Utah Medical Center to interview about a residency, Greg had managed to stop for a visit, taking a cab from the Salt Lake Airport without any idea about how far (and how expensive) it would be. He had arrived at our house while Stel was at a vet's, and when she returned home, she found this intense young man waiting, being entertained by Cory's practice on his trumpet, and curious to know what kind of animal had dug all those elaborate burrows in our hillside (answer: a rare Matthew's badger).

An hour before, Stel had been arguing with Dr.Collier over an eagle, which had a clean break in its leg. Dr.C. had insisted on casting the bird with its leg stretched straight. Stel said she believed the ankle joint and patella should be left to stretch. He assured her it would not hyperextend, but by the time she reached home with the bird, it was bleeding, cutting its leg against the cast.

Greg agreed it might be a problem, and he helped her pad the cast and remove part of it. Then we spent a pleasant day and a half exchanging theories, experience and stories, establishing a friendship. Greg went to his U. of U. interviews, and we bid good-bye for the time being.

A few weeks later, the cast came off the eagle Dr.Collier had worked on, and true to Stel's concern, the patella was hyperextended, and the foot had rotated to a grotesque angle. The bird would have no grip in that foot so Dr. Collier suggested amputation, which seemed to be the only course left. Stel had X rays taken, then put Dr.Collier on hold and shipped the pictures to Greg Ivins.

"Ship the eagle to me," he said via long distance, minutes after he had viewed the X rays. Another money quandary: we were already into the eagle a bundle with Dr. C's vet fees, and shipping would be more. What was important? Money? A life? My priorities were getting better by the moment, and we shipped the bird with little hesitation, the first of many birds we sent to Greg, some of them compliments of Delta Air Lines once they learned of Stel's work. With Steve Stohl, a veterinarian in Columbia, Greg set about reconstructing the tendon for "Junior," Greg's name for the eagle. He rebroke and reset the bone and realigned the ankle joint, and for good measure he and Stohl discovered a hitherto undescribed tendon in the legs of golden eagles. ("The eagle knew it was there all the time," said Stel pungently as Greg excitedly described the find on the phone.)

A few weeks after surgery, the eagle went from 25 percent function in the leg to 95 percent, and just to make certain Junior was fit and ready for release, Greg exercised him daily. When he was certain the bird was okay, Greg released Junior in western Missouri, where he was last seen heading toward Kansas at four hundred feet and climbing. "I practice on people so I can do birds," Greg added, a twinkle in his voice, after describing the release.

Greg is a passionate bird lover and a falconer, specializing in hawking with accipiters. In college he karyotyped kestrels—using them because the sexes were visually apparent. Greg and Dr. William Halliwell eventually researched and published baselines for elements contained in the blood of raptors, enabling others to compare them to see what was normal. Greg kept eagles as blood donors and learned that eagle blood can be accepted by buteos such as red-tails at least once, and also by other species of eagles.

Today Greg Ivins conducts orthopedic surgery and organ transplants in humans but still has time for his falconry and raptor research. He lives in Fulton, Missouri.

Eventually a fine veterinarian arrived on the local scene, packaged in a gruff, round exterior, topped by sandy red hair with a matching beard. His name was Ross Anderson and he had been hired by a large local dog-and-cat clinic, famous for a billing schedule which starts where the Mayo Clinic tops out.

"I think this guy is pretty good," said one of the falconers after an emergency run to the clinic. "I mean, like he *owns* his own birds—parrots 'n' stuff," added the hip falconer.

Ever wary but hopeful, Stel trucked into Ross with a bird and discovered, to her delight, that he was what we had been looking for all along. "He moves like a bird person—soft, slow and easy," Stel reported happily that evening.

Later Ross left the clinic to head veterinary services for Hogle Zoo in Salt Lake, and his management graciously volunteered his time to us, providing the best of all worlds: free vet service from a qualified, committed professional who loves birds. The zoo and aviary have supplied X rays, treatment and care, and Ross is not afraid to say "I don't know," or to refer a bird that needs special attention he cannot offer.

I am glad to say much has changed in veterinary care since these hesitant, early experiences. As von Blucher said as he led the Russians at Leipzig in 1813, "Ever forward, but slowly."

A falconer's adult female peregrine—fat, healthy, in fine plumage. Falconers provided much of the knowledge about birds of prey. (Photo by Ray O. Kirkland)

12

CONTRIBUTIONS OF FALCONRY

Tradition cannot be inherited, and if you want it you must obtain it by great labor.
—T. S. ELIOT

Treatment of a falcon led to our first encounter with a falconer; the bird, a tiercel prairie falcon, was given up to us by its holder and slowly died due to what probably was parasites. We soon realized that falconry was very important to our project, since knowledge about the behavior and the physiology of birds of prey was almost entirely the province of falconers.

Other birds were brought by falconers regularly, at first out of pride so we might see what a *real* trained falcon was, including several illegal peregrines and merlins, since the Migratory Bird Act, which banned the taking of certain birds for falconry, had just been passed by the federal government. But soon the reasons for their coming were reversed. They came because they needed medical-treatment information from Stel, or they came as malefactors to visit the birds that had been taken from them for various violations of state or federal law. These included everything from failure to obtain a falconry license to trapping birds out of season.

What enigmatic men (and a few women) these falconers were! On the one hand, they were taking birds from the wild, which triggered in me a certain amount of philosophical friction. (Yet I was *killing* ducks, I was gently reminded one night. They were only *taking* falcons, and many of these escaped back to the wild, was the rationale I was given. As for *taking* falcons that *killed* ducks, I was reminded that was what the falcon did in the wild anyway.)

On the other hand, these same falconers were vigorous in their efforts to conserve birds of prey, and virtually all medical and behavioral knowledge of raptors had come from the fount of falconry, passed down since the first Arab rolled a red-eyed goshawk out of a rug four thousand years before Christ. It was in the Orient and Middle East that falconry got its start, and today it is to the privileged Arab what baseball is to Americans.

Hunting with hawks has never been an efficient means of providing food. It is an art requiring the luxury of leisure or the pressure of necessity, and it may have been a reasonable means of providing meat for the Arab's pot as he traveled from wadi to wadi, protein being scarce (at least it is today) in the Middle East. Arabs and Orientals fully developed the art, and it reached its efflorescence during medieval times. Marco Polo wrote of a Manchurian ruler who engaged ten thousand men to care for his one thousand falcons.

It took the remarkable early-day biologist/regent, Frederick II of Hohenstaufen, king of Sicily and Jerusalem and emperor of the Holy Roman Empire, to formalize and codify falconry in his book written about A.D.1250, *De Arte Venandi cum Avibus (The Art of Falconry)*. Some argue that it was the sophisticated and highly intellectual court life of Frederick that marked the first soaring flight of the Italian Renaissance, Savonarola yet lurking with slings and arrows in the gloomy ambushes of the future.

Frederick, for reasons that differ from ours, always put the bird first (human life was cheap). On falconers and their qualifications, he says:

He who would be fully instructed in falconry must be proficient in the feeding, the attendance upon training, and the domestication of falcons, and in teaching them how to catch their quarry.

The falconer should be of medium size . . . he ought to be moderately fleshy, so that he is not handicapped by emaciation and thus unable to do hard work or to withstand cold; nor should he be fat so that he is likely to shun exertion . . . he must be diligent so that as old age approaches he will still pursue the sport out of a pure love of it. For as the cultivation of an art is long and new methods are constantly introduced, a man may bring the art itself nearer to perfection.

Frederick rails against drunkenness, bad eyesight, gluttony and deafness as detrimental to the falconer, and encourages him to be able to "swim across unfordable water and follow his bird when she has flown over and requires assistance." He then goes on to observe:

A bad temper is a grave failing. A falcon may frequently commit acts that provoke the anger of her keeper, and unless he has his temper strictly under control he may indulge in improper acts toward a sensitive bird so that she will very soon be ruined.

Frederick knew birds: they cannot be worked like dogs or horses. A bird person can only work *with* the bird, never against it, never willfully, never harshly, although one falconer I know taps his bird on the back to show displeasure, and the female prairie falcon he flies seems to understand the gesture.

Frederick also provides explicit instructions on training, medical treatment, hoods and mews, and a thousand other details about hawks, including the kind of dessert they should be treated to: butter balls rolled in sugar. So involved was Frederick in his birds, in fact, that he lost a battle because he was hawking, not tending to war.

Avibus is still looked to as the Bible of falconry, in spite of scientific advances that include telemetry, which may relieve a falconer from the necessity of swimming the aforementioned unfordable water. (I add, however, that I have witnessed Steve Chindgren swim unfordable waterways several times, some choked with January ice, in order to reach a hawk on a kill.)

As falconry's popularity grew, royalty were assigned falcons according to the order of nobility: only the king or emperor could fly a gyrfalcon, the peregrine was reserved for princes, and merlins and kestrels went to lesser nobles and ladies. This pecking order (excuse the pun) was used as a means of determining taxes and paying creditors by nobility in medieval England. One legal settlement adjudged the loser to pay "one hundred Norway Hawks and one hundred Girfals." During the reign of James I in the early seventeenth century, Sir Thomas Monson paid one thousand pounds for two gyrfalcons, a lot of money, especially then.

There were reasons for this system: the gyrfalcon is desirable because it is large and powerful, capable of taking most prey through a tail chase. The peregrine is the premier aerialist of the world, able to capture even swifts and swallows, yet big enough to capture game like grouse, and when flown in pairs, called a "cast," capable of bringing down very large birds such as herons. Merlins are a delight to watch in flight, offering stunning maneuverability. Since they are smaller, their prey is limited. Kestrels were at the bottom of the order, their name coming from "costril," meaning "milksop, white liver, craven, one that cannot say boo to a goose"—which is anything but true of our North American kestrel, a jaunty, fearless true falcon with which I have had enormous fun when I flew them on grasshoppers in the manner of the Chinese.

In North America we have one other falcon of note, the prairie falcon, a fast, flat-out flyer used to feeding in many areas on ground dwellers, but capable of sterling aerobatics when trained or determined.

For many years the Din family of Pakistan provided all the hawks that the falconers of the Middle East and Europe could use, selling a tiercel peregrine for as little as fifty dollars. If he did not sell, he went into the cooking pot, or was sold to an herbalist for medicine. (In China thousands of hawks are eaten by humans each year.)

Shakespeare wrote sonnets and plays laced with references to falconry, "give her the slip" being but one example of a falconry phrase common in his plays. A "slip" is the release of a falcon so it may commence chasing its quarry.

From the heights of Frederick and Shakespeare to shooting hawks as vermin took less than three hundred years, since to kill a falcon in medieval times was once a crime punishable by death. In the nineteenth and twentieth centuries, people were paid to kill them as nuisances—until about 1920 when a study in Pennsylvania found that it cost far more to pay bounties on hawks than the value of the poultry being lost to them (a parallel similar to the sheep/coyote situation in the West today, according to the "Wagner Report," a Utah State University—coordinated study in the 1970s).

The practice of falconry had virtually died out by the nineteenth century, though the English, who have developed similar anachronisms to a high art, managed to keep it alive. By the twentieth century, it was all but gone even in England, the times not being either interested or patient enough to deal with the "craftsmanship" required of falconry.

And in America? "I feel that one cannot confidently recommend a course of falconry to our friends across the Atlantic," wrote English falconer Gilbert Blaine early in the twentieth century. "They would want to learn the whole bag of tricks in less than two months," he stated.

Falconry eventually did take a small hold in the U.S., the first articles on it appearing in popular literature in the 1920s and '30s (the famous grizzly bear and raptor researchers, John and Frank Craighead, were among the early falconers featured in articles such as those run by *National Geographic*). Today there are about twenty-five hundred licensed master falconers in the U.S., according to the North American Falconer's Association, along with a few hundred general and apprentice falconers.

I have found many misconceptions among those who have never watched a trained falcon work at game hawking, so here is a short course.

All falcons and hawks are hawks, but not all hawks are falcons. Following me? Hawks are accipiters—goshawks, Cooper's hawks and sharp-shinned hawks; they are short winged, and long tailed, the drag racers of birds of prey, capable of quick flights from the fist after fast-rising or running prey. These are maneuverable forest dwellers. A person who flies these hawks is called an *austringer*, and he flies them from the fist, releasing them as the bunny zigs away or the quail rises from the brush pile.

Buteos—soaring hawks—are flown by some falconers, and particularly popular are red-tailed hawks, flown from horseback in some areas of the country, especially California, where owners may give their birds a bit of dash by suspending the eye of a peacock feather on fine thread over the rich russet of the bird's tail. Red-tails are usually "flown on" cottontail rabbits or jackrabbits.

There is another hawk, a parabuteo called a Harris' hawk, that is also popular with falconers. A bird of the Sonoran Desert, it is flown on both ground and flighted creatures, and is highly desired for its affectionate nature and its intelligence.

Falcons—called long wings—are flown by falconers. Quarry is usually sighted on the ground, perhaps found by pointers or setters trained to work with falcons. The quarry sought by falconers is always avian, and the prey holds to the ground as the falcon is released to "ring up" higher and higher in the sky. At last the falcon reaches a "pitch" or good position high above, and then the falconer moves in to flush the quarry. The quarry rises, and the falcon drops in a spectacular steep dive, called a "stoop," and nicks the duck, pheasant or sage grouse with its talon or foot, usually sending the bird tumbling from the sky. The falcon then does a "wingover" and settles on its prey on the ground, commencing to bite the bird's head or neck to kill it.

As the bird is doing this, the falconer must walk or run to the falcon and its prey, and "make into" them, picking them both up on his fist as the falcon eats. He secures the jesses on the feet of the falcon, lets it eat, then hoods it. To the many who ask, "Doesn't the falcon retrieve the pheasant?" the answer is no. The falconer retrieves both falcon and pheasant.

Falconry can be a very pleasant pastime as locating quarry often consists of driving back roads on golden autumn and frosty wintery days, noting game movements, listening to music in the warmth of the vehicle, and watching flights of ducks and geese weave above the nodding cattails. At the end lies a proper slip, away from fences, dangerous power lines, and falcon-killing eagles, with perhaps a pintail to put in the bag after the falcon has been hooded. As the sun drops through the mists over Great Salt Lake, the falconer toasts his bird with a small glass of fine cream sherry to warm the tummy, for there are many men of style among those who fly falcons. That is the ideal end of the ideal falconry day; behind it lie arduous months of daily training to prepare for that heart-stopping ten-second stoop.

Months before, the falconer decides what kind of bird he will fly, and that is dictated by the terrain, the availability of game and how far he is able to travel to fly his bird. A long wing should be flown every day; a short wing may be flown irregularly (weekend goshawking or red-tail hawking. Most serious falconers I know work morning jobs and are off and hawking by 2:00 P.M. winter afternoons, or they may not work at all in winter, letting a wife carry the economic load, or working many hours at construction jobs in summer in exchange for winter freedom.)

The falconer buys his bird—say, a tiercel peregrine—from a captive breeder at a cost of five hundred dollars. This is a small peregrine, but since the falconer lives not too far from small ditches and farm ponds in a flat, relatively risk-free area where many teal and shoveler ducks are found, he deems this bird his best choice. Another falconer might select a large female peregrine or a hybrid peregrine-gyrfalcon cross to fly after pintails or mallards or sage grouse, and currently might pay as much as two thousand dollars for his bird.

Certain birds may be taken from the nest or trapped as passage or adult birds, but there are heavy restrictions on what may be taken and how. No peregrines may be taken from the wild, and restrictions on gyrfalcons are so severe as to make them effectively available only to Alaskan and Canadian falconers. Accipiters are regularly taken as nestlings, as are prairie falcons in some western states. Most birds in falconry today are captive bred.

Once the falconer has his bird, training begins. Conditioning is done by giving or withholding food—giving food to provide positive reinforcement, withholding food to create in the bird the desire to hunt. The bird is first flown to the fist for food; then the distance is increased. Next the bird is flown on a *creance*, or long line, always being returned to the fist to eat. Then comes the art of hooding, which is the mark of excellence in a hawk person; hooding keeps the bird calm and quiet for transporting.

Once this has been done, the bird may be flown on a pigeon or a lure, and a good falconer will watch every subtle move of the bird, reinforcing the falcon by building its confidence, urging it ever higher, or encouraging fearlessness with game even larger than itself. This cannot be done through starvation or force; it can only be done through love of the bird, patience and minute observation of behavior.

Steve Chindgren has "built" a twenty-six-ounce falcon to a point where it readily and fearlessly captures "flying cinder blocks," the chunky, fast, five-pound northern Utah sage grouse, a match even for eagles. It is this finesse and polish that separate a good falconer from a fine falconer, the latter always reaching for the apogee of the art.

And what finally happens to falconry birds? I know of no surveys, but I believe most are lost to the wild. This creates some very interesting and far-reaching questions, since fertile eggs have been noted in some first-generation, captive-bred hybrid falcons. This implies that escaped hybrids may breed with wild birds. Yet hybrids are not uncommon among some bird species, especially ducks. What might happen to the gene pool? Only long-term observation will tell us.

"I lost my bird; keep an ear open for anyone who might bring it in" was our oft-heard lament from the falconers. Many birds found their way to us, and many were returned to their holders. (I hesitate to say owners, because no human can own a wild thing.) But many birds sailed north on hormone-warming breezes, and others, fed and fat, simply had no reason to continue their liaison with the humans who had provided their food. As fickle as cats they are, for I have heard the laughter of departing hawks.

I do know that painstaking falconers like Chindgren keep a single, well-trained bird for many years through careful falconry practices and the unswerving use and knowledge of telemetry. Falcons often meet accidental deaths, just as they might in the wild. Steve (and others I know) have lost birds to power-line electrocutions, great horned owls, eagles, and fences and automobiles which they have struck. A few falcons also go to breeding projects to live out their golden years happily raising babies.

Perhaps the odds for a falcon are better in captivity than in the wild, as raptor people generally accept the aforementioned figure of 80 percent loss among young wild falcons during the first year of their life. I can make a strong case for a high survival rate among falcons trained to hunt which are lost by falconers.

Falconers have come under a barrage of criticism from those who believe the art should be outlawed.

"But who else really *cares* about birds of prey?" asks falconer Chindgren, multitime award winner of the North American Falconer's Association field meets. "Who else has worked to get laws to protect them? We love the birds."

Ducks Unlimited members create habitat for ducks so they can shoot them, but in the process provide great benefits for more than just ducks. So it is with falconers, and they do not consciously kill falcons. Many falconers are on the cutting edge of bird-of-prey research: Tom Cade, the peregrine man from Cornell, the Peregrine Fund and the World Center for Birds of Prey in Boise; taxonomist and ecologist Clayton White of Brigham Young University, one of the men who enabled America to list the *anatum* peregrine as endangered; the Hammerstroms, Richard Fyfe of Canada, and Richard "Butch" Olendorff of the Bureau of Land Management; Jim Ruos, formerly of the Fish and Wildlife Service; Frank Bond, a New Mexico state legislator; Pat Redig, the raptor veterinarian with the University of Minnesota; Jim Enderson, a professor at Colorado College and possibly the first to captive-breed peregrines; Bill Burnham, with the World Center for Birds of Prey and the Peregrine Fund, who is dedicated and hardworking, pumping out hundreds of birds for reintroduction; and there are the younger, hot falconers like Pat Benson, now researching in Africa, and Steve Platt, formerly raptor biologist with Black Butte Coal, now with the Wyoming Department of Environmental Quality. I could name many others.

And mother-henning and cudgeling all to make certain birds of prey get the attention they deserve is Morlan Nelson, the guru falconer, a persona so strong that he can knock heads together by the power of his voice alone. He gets attention for birds of prey and somehow has been the man who "wakes the morning" for them.

Our association with falconers imbued us with the peregrine mystique. Falconers who had flown this bird were eloquent in their description of its flight, its behavior and its response to proper handling. It is, as they said, a sexy bird, treasured for its beautiful markings—boldly defined with dark blue-blacks, rakish sideburns called malers, and beautiful pencilings and dottings on a peach breast. Add huge yellow feet, and a very large, liquid, dark eye, and you have a hopelessly stunning bird found the world over in twenty-six different races (or if you are a lumper, not a splitter, in its single race with regional variations. Arguments will be raging on this issue for years to come, and only genetic "fingerprinting" research may finally settle the question.)

Falconers and bird watchers love the peregrine for its speed and dash. This account of its vaunted speed is from 1930, as observed by an "expert aviator":

> He was flying a small pursuit plane, which had a normal speed of about 125 miles per hour and, while cruising about at a considerable altitude, he saw a bunch of ducks flying far below and ahead of him. Thinking to gain some experience in diving at a moving object, he turned the nose down and opened the throttle of his engine, thereby gaining speed rapidly. While he was still some distance from the ducks he glanced at the wingtip of his plane to see how much vibration his swoop was causing and as he did so, a hawk "shot by him as though the plane was standing still," and struck one of the ducks which fell towards the ground apparently lifeless. At the time the hawk passed the plane the latter was traveling at a speed of nearly 175 miles an hour . . . the hawk was perhaps not far from double that rate.[8]

Joseph A. Hagar, a Massachusetts state ornithologist quoted in Bent, experienced the thrill of the falconer during his 1935–36 season with peregrines:

> . . . eventually the patient watcher will see an exhibition of flying that is literally breath-taking . . . We were hidden in the woods below the south end of the cliff, and the peregrines were quite unconscious of our presence at the time; again and again the tercel started well to leeward and came along the cliff against the wind, diving, plunging, saw-toothing, rolling over and over, darting hither and yon like an autumn leaf until finally he would swoop up into the full current of air and be borne off on the gale to do it all

over again. At length he tired of this and soaring in narrow circles without any movement of his wings other than a constant small adjustment of their planes, he rose to a position 500 or 600 feet above the mountain and north of the cliff. Nosing over suddenly, he flicked his wings rapidly fifteen or twenty times and fell like a thunderbolt. Wings half closed now, he shot down past the north end of the cliff, described three successive vertical loop-the-loops across its face, turning completely upside down at the top of each loop, and roared out over our heads with the wind rushing like ripping canvas.[9]

One June night, a call came to Stellanie from the UDWR, which had been in touch with the U.S. Park Service at Lake Powell in southern Utah. Two fishermen at Lone Rock, near Wahweap, had watched a hovering helicopter blow a smallish, brown hawk into the water. They had picked it up and had taken it to park headquarters.

By now the UDWR had appointed a raptor biologist, a handsome, mustachioed distance runner with a fey sense of humor named Phillip Wagner, who now told Stellanie the arriving bird "might be on the endangered list." There was only one bird on the endangered list that matched that description: a peregrine.

Phil had sent a UDWR biologist named Tom Boner to get the bird, and Boner was on his way to our house so Stel could check it over and provide shelter and food until a determination on what to do with it could be made. There was unconcealed excitement in Phil's voice, and Matt and Cory were jumping with exhilaration at the prospect that we might get to see a wild peregrine youngster.

I was skeptical; for some time we had regularly received calls from well-meaning citizens who had found "peregrines." When I picked them up, they ran the gamut from kestrels to owls, proving only that while folks care, they don't necessarily have their identifications down pat. Never had we received a real peregrine.

The bird had been the subject of much study and interest as its numbers declined, due in part to DDT that thinned eggshells, a fact learned through a comparison with nineteenth-century peregrine eggs in egg collections. At one point in the early 1970s, the USF&WS issued a press release saying that only fifty-three known pairs of *anatum* peregrines were nesting in the contiguous forty-eight states; this was cited as one of the reasons for declaring the bird endangered, but it did prompt a war cry from some falconers who said the *tundrius* race of the bird was still very abundant in Alaska and Canada, and it also set off a scientific tussle. The USF&WS ruled that to protect *anatum* all races had to be protected. Some said there was only one race (the lumpers previously mentioned), and even today there are revisionists among falconers and biologists.

In reaction to this attention, peregrine breeding facilities began pumping out young peregrines for reintroduction to areas where they had formerly been abundant.

That night we waited expectantly. Wagner came to our house, anticipating the bird's arrival. "Oh, it just *can't* be a peregrine, it just *can't* be one," he kept saying, fearful not only of dealing with the sensitive bird (he was new on the job), but also intimidated by the blizzard of paperwork that would doubtless be entailed.

Lights showed in the driveway about 11:00 P.M.; it was Tom Boner, and he carried a cardboard box into the house. Stel took the box from Tom and placed it on the kitchen counter. Stel, Phil, Tom, Cory, Matt and Jim peered down as the box was opened.

Two brown eyes looked up at us fearlessly. Some silly sprigs of down waved from the top of the dark brown head, and the beak was half open, more out of curiosity, it seemed to me, than of fear. There were very dark sideburns on the bird's cheeks, and large, spidery, blue-green feet that would later turn butter yellow. He cackled at us softly and even the sound was different from other falcons we had held. There was a long pause as Stel looked the bird over. "It's a peregrine," said Stel, letting her breath out.

"My God, it's a peregrine," said Phil and Tom as one.

"A peregrine, a peregrine," said Cory and Matt, almost reverently.

Stel picked the bird up as if it were a filament, delicate and breakable. The little headdress of down bobbed and breezed as the youngster kicked his big feet in resistance. Stel palpated the bird carefully and slowly. Not a word was spoken until she was finished.

"No breaks, swellings or other indications of external problems," said Stel. I could tell she was in awe not only of the bird, but of the expectations of the state and federal wildlife agencies. What if something should go wrong? What if something went undetected? What if the bird died on her?

I imagined what was going through her mind at the moment, which she later confirmed. Outwardly she pursed her lips and looked the pro. I was overwhelmed by the presence of the bird. "You're holding approximately 1 percent of the known *anatum* peregrines in the forty-eight states," I said.

Calls were quickly placed to Morlan Nelson in Boise; he was out, but his son, Tyler, a raptor pro in his own right, would call back. Al Heggen was at a meeting in Phoenix. Jim Hogue, our federal agent, was out on an assignment. No one in authority could be reached. What to do with this bird?

Stel decided to feed and hydrate the little fellow, and she prepared a batch of her mix, which she gently squeezed down the bird's throat. The bird was then placed in a mews chamber, and we all had a glass of Riesling, for the nerves, of course.

At dawn the calls started coming, and I faced the phone somewhat blearily, my tongue fuzzy from the night's postperegrine revelry. Stellanie soon was answering questions, mostly from Hogue, who would confer with USF&WS in Washington to see what was to be done with the bird. As soon as he had placed his calls, Hogue was off like a shot to Lake Powell to try to find the helicopter that had washed the little bird from his nest—the first known peregrine eyrie in Utah since the late 1950s.

The big question now was what would become of the bird? It could be used to beef up the genetic pool of those peregrines being used in captive breeding; it could go back to its eyrie on Lake Powell, if the eyrie was reasonably undisturbed and the adults were still there.

Calls came from individuals offering "help" by providing a place where the bird could be put on display for the public (and for their profit); we also got calls from a private captive breeder who wanted the bird. Amazing, I thought, how quickly the word spreads.

After much conferring, Stel suggested the bird go to the Peregrine Fund and its reintroduction program of captive breeding, then being conducted at Fort Collins, Colorado. Wagner agreed, along with the USF&WS.

An hour later, Stel received a call from Bill Burnham, the previously mentioned falconer and manager of the Peregrine Fund's breeding operation: he wanted the bird and he was very concerned about it, especially since it was in the hands of an amateur, and a woman at that. Burnham did not know us or our operation, and his exposure to other rehabilitators had been typical: he was unimpressed by what he had seen. It would be at least twenty-four hours before he could have the bird picked up by someone he trusted. "What kinds of birds have you had?" he asked bluntly.

"Eagles, prairie falcons. Lots of owls. Marsh hawks. Some accipiters—" Stel was sharply interrupted.

"What kind of accipiters?" he asked.

"All three—goshawks, Cooper's, sharp-shins. Most recently I had a sharp-shin that came with a dinged wing and a concussion. It had probably hit a window," she said.

"What did you feed it and how did you treat it?" Burnham asked.

"We fed it chicken and small birds. I left it alone in a box to heal," Stel said.

"And what happened to it?"

"I released it," Stel said.

Burnham relaxed. He knew that sharpies are the most difficult birds of all to handle. He figured if Stel could do that, she could do a peregrine. "I feel like I've arrived," Stel said later.

A letter from the USF&WS instructed her to transfer the bird, and arrangements were made the next day to fly the peregrine to Fort

Collins from Salt Lake, hand carried by a Peregrine Fund staffer.

I often marvel at how a little brown bird with goofy-looking sprigs of down on his head could send such a ripple through the bureaucracies. If the events had taken place just a few years before, none of this apparatus would ever have cared about the little guy. It was good that times were changing, that the country was beginning to care about its critters.

Next day the youngster was perched high in the mews, looking down as we entered. He did not bate or fly; he simply watched calmly, curiously, as only peregrines do. Stel placed a quail on the perch. He focused on it, sidled over to it, then plumed the bird as if we were not there.

In a minute he had finished his meal and was feaking on the perch. In a day he was in Colorado, and in three years he was fathering the first of many dozens of peregrines that would be released to the wild, all the result of centuries of knowledge acquired by falconers.

Rodriguez Carter, a young red-tail, bound into Stellanie's face, sinking talons into her eye socket. (Photo by Stellanie Ure)

13

The Heat Of Conflict

Laws are like cobwebs which
may catch small flies but let
wasps and hornets break
through.

—Jonathan Swift

Some falconers we met were rascals, just as there are in any group, but it was hard to discern which ones were malefactors. They all offered kindness and help. One man particularly was respected for his knowledge, and on first meeting, he looked familiar. His name was Bill and he brought the hawks gifts of food, leashes, jesses, hoods and bells.

He was solicitous of Stel, in part because of her size, and warned her several times to take care in dealing with imprinted eyas birds, saying they could redirect their behavior in ways that could hurt a human. At the time we had several young red-tails perched in the yard, and one evening as Stel was feeding, "a fury slinging flame" sunk his talons into her eye and lip. Of course blood filled the eye instantly as the imprinted red-tailed hawk, named Rodriguez Carter (from the *nom de plume* of a friend and writer), clung to Stel's face like a psychopathic horror.

"I've been hit," I heard Stel cry from the far side of the driveway. The bird was still clinging to her face when I reached my stride, both kids on my heels. She reached up and got a grip on the bird's neck, as she had been told to do by Bill in case of an emergency, and the hawk released its claws. She threw the bird back at its perch and faced us, blood streaming from her eye and cheek.

Stel cursed herself for not having been more circumspect with the bird; maybe it was overconfidence, maybe just laxity. "Bill warned me, and warned me, and warned me about these screamers," she said. (Eyas birds tend to scream. The Arabs do not like them and call them "mad hawks.")

"You think I might have learned," she lamented as I wiped the blood from around her eye. We were quickly in the car, heading for the emergency room at St. Mark's Hospital three miles away. To console her, I told her the story of being bitten by a bobcat while working for Disney, and then of being bitten by a ground squirrel while on a film location.

"You didn't have your eye put out," she cried, holding a gauze pad over the injury. The kids were absolutely quiet in the backseat as we raced for the hospital. "I think I can see," Stel finally said, blinking through the blood. I could hear the relief in her voice.

We pulled into the emergency room in record time and within minutes, an old acquaintance, Dr. Corkery, had taken Stel into an examining room. Cory had been to Dr. Corkery for what we thought might be broken ribs from a school wrestling match; Matthew had dinged his elbow in a fall on ice and he, too, had been examined by Corkery. In each case the doctor had asked them and me very pointed questions to determine if their father or mother was abusing them.

"Uh, I can see now," Stel said hopefully after a few minutes with the doctor. The talon had sliced between the bony socket and the eye, going in cleanly without damage to the eye itself. Blood had gotten between her iris and her contact lens. Tissue was crushed and cut, but Stel's eye would be fine. Her lip gash needed a stitch or two, and now she was more concerned about the cosmetics of the aftermath.

"Did he do this to you?" asked Corkery, pointing to me. "Did he do this to her?" he asked the children separately as my mouth dropped.

"Rodriguez Carter did it," said Matthew.

"Who is he?"

"A red-tailed hawk."

"Do you expect me to believe that?"

"It's true," said Stel. I was nodding my head in vigorous assent, and my eyes must have been as big as saucers.

Corkery looked at the kids, probably remembering vaguely that they had been among the thousands he treats each year in the E.R. I was glad he was thorough and conscientious, but it was nonetheless a discomfiting feeling to stand accused of abusing my wife. Look at those wounds; did he think I had used an ice pick, turkey skewers, a stiletto?

"It was my fault," said Stel on the way home. "I should have listened to Bill. I can't blame the bird. The hawk is the way he is, and Rodriguez Carter was made psychotic by his previous handler early in his life."

The next day a UDWR worker secured a court order for the release of Rodriguez Carter in record time (and on a Saturday), and we were permitted to release the bird (it had been confiscated for being illegally taken).

The drama was not quite over. We drove to an isolated area near the mouth of Big Cottonwood Canyon about three minutes from home. We had released birds there before. I picked Carter out of the cardboard box, allowing time for Stel to shoot a couple of photos before releasing him. I tossed the bird gently into the wind. A few flaps and he caught a southerly gust, circling overhead once, twice— and then he folded his wings and dived at Stel, growing ever larger in her camera viewfinder until she dropped to the ground in terror and disbelief.

Carter whooshed by a foot or two over her head, gained altitude, and flew to the north until out of sight. "I certainly know how their prey feels at the last moment," Stel said.

Bill came to the house the same day, genuinely angry at Stel for not heeding his warnings. We listened as he talked about some of his experiences, and in the course of the conversation, we learned that our youthful paths had crossed at Disney Studios—he had been a trapper, I had been a trainer. His knowledge was excellent and I bade him to return.

Bill then stopped by regularly, bringing with him some of his friends, including Dean, a somewhat tarnished memory from my Disney days. Dean had stolen Rick and Sam, two baby raccoons, from the studio compound. Dean, too, had been just a kid then, and now he was into hawks.

There were other friends of Bill, amiable men, but as I got to know them, I realized they shared a cynicism, even a hatred, for the laws and those who enforced them. It was also apparent they had no respect for life. By now thoroughly comfortable, Bill illustrated with glee for me how he and the others had been involved in planned deceptions of wildlife workers:

The U.S. Air Force is unaware that it was the victim of one of Bill's scams—a switch in falcons destined for use in starling control on a southern Air Force base. After much expense and effort to obtain eyas Peale's peregrines (the largest of all the races of peregrine, and one of the most desirable for falconry) from the Queen Charlotte Islands, an inside man carefully coordinated a switch in the shipment. The Air Force received young prairie falcons and was never aware of the difference, since either bird is suitable for airport control. But for those falconers to whom the Peale's peregrines were distributed, it was the classic against which all other bird scams were measured.

Bill's friends, Wally and Squirt, climbed onto California's famous Morro Rock peregrine eyrie one night during the breeding season in the mid-1970s. Members of the Audubon Society, attempting to protect the eyrie, were maintaining a twenty-four-hour vigil. They had even been warned by other falconers that an attempt on the nest would be made. Wally and Squirt roped into the eyrie in darkness, and two young peregrines were taken beneath the noses of the watchers. (The birds were later recovered when an informer told wildlife lawmen of their whereabouts.)

Bill himself willingly swapped and sold any bird, reptile or mammal he could get—from Scottish merlins to peregrines and goshawks. He took orders for them, undaunted by the fact that the new wildlife laws forbade it. "Laws are for others" was his operating motto.

"Want a parrot?" he asked. Bill's medical-student friend smuggled hundreds over the Mexican border by rolling them in sleeping bags. If inspected, the evidence could be unrolled, they thought, and the evidence would fly off. It did not work that way when the plan was finally put into practice, however, for many of the parrots had smothered in the bag. An arrest was made, but the fine was so nominal that it did not act as a deterrent.

Bill and his friends were into falconry and wildlife vandalism just for the excitement of the scam. To be chased by law enforcers was a necessary part of the experience for them. He crowed about beating the law by publishing an eight-page newsletter called *The Poach Report*, a copy of which I kept. The names were changed to protect the guilty. There were articles on poaching trout in fish hatcheries, trapping ducks, shooting gulls, using mist nets to trap doves, and using radio telephones to report the whereabouts of conservation officers while Bill and his friends were poaching.

Bill several times urged me or Stel to take a peregrine or a Harris' hawk he offered, but we feared they would be illegal and that might entangle or obligate us.

Finally, after providing us with so much information and material, he popped the question: would we allow him to launder illegal birds through the rehabilitation project? The answer was no, and after that, his visits were few and far between.

Often we received falconers' birds from state or federal officers after a bust, and the result was that the falconer sometimes visited to make certain his bird was being treated properly, since cases abounded in which confiscated birds were either killed and frozen or turned over to inept, unknowledgeable or uncaring rehabilitators. Falconers are as passionate about their birds as parents are about children; sometimes it felt like visiting day at the delinquency hall.

One young falconer of about seventeen was on our doorstep less than an hour after his beautiful, immature female goshawk had been delivered to us by state officers. With him came food, a good perch and an offer of any assistance we desired. He wanted to make certain his bird was properly cared for. He smoldered with bird passion and eventually he got his hawk back.

Another young man whose prairie falcon had been taken threatened to use a gun to get his bird back, making Stel very uncomfortable. Stel took him on a tour of our facilities and explained in detail how the falcon would be fed, protected and perched. Slowly his mood shifted; he became a supporter and friend until his untimely death from AIDS a few years later.

One day the state brought two young, docile, sweet-mannered red-tails, explaining they had been confiscated from a happy family. The children of the family had painted the birds' talons with Scarlet Peach fingernail polish by Max Factor.

A large luxury car soon pulled into the driveway, disgorging a family led by a man looking quite familiar . . . curly hair, a flash of a gold tooth . . . Dean of Disney theft days! His children and wife strolled around the grounds as Dean talked with Stel and me at the mews.

Within a week one of the toenail-painted birds was stolen from the project, and whoever took it left behind a dozen freshly killed green-winged teal—kind of an offering-in-lieu. We suspected it was Dean liberating his bird, but why did he not take both of them? Later, when Stel confronted him, he did not deny taking the bird: he just grinned that flashy gold tooth.

There was one attempt on the mews late at night, when I was out of town. Stel heard a car pull up and a door slam about 3:00 A.M. In pajamas and waving a flashlight, she first called the sheriff, then yelled that the sheriff was on the way. A scampering sound was followed by the slamming of car doors and the roaring of a car engine. Stel spent an uncomfortable remainder of the evening.

During the first years after the passage of the Migratory Bird Act, aimed at curbing the taking of all birds, saving the peregrine, and establishing falconry laws, wildlife lawmen were handicapped by their lack of knowledge about birds of prey. Men like Bill could tell a "game warden," as he called him, that a peregrine falcon was a sharp-shinned hawk, and he would not know the difference. Time and again we received misidentified birds and Stellanie would gently encourage the conservation officer to "look at the *whole* bird."

A person who had spent twenty years identifying waterfowl suddenly had to become a hawk expert, and they often came to us with bird in one hand, field guide in the other. We received birds misidentified as a goshawk (really a red-tail), a gyrfalcon (a rough-legged hawk), and peregrines (prairie falcons, Cooper's hawks, kestrels and sharp-shins).

The scene was further confused by the fact that peregrines held by falconers prior to the passage of the Migratory Bird Act were legal to keep—as long as the new plastic falconry bands were put on the birds. There were abuses, since many falconers rushed out and presented freshly trapped birds for banding, saying they had had them for several years. Falconry bands were also counterfeited, but lawmen had expected that there would be some calumny, and built in the "fudge factor" that recognized they couldn't totally control violations.

Meanwhile each state had to promulgate falconry laws guided by the federal regulations; in Utah falconers like Terry Roundy helped the state develop fair laws and a falconry test that could be administered to all falconers and would-bes. Some states—Oregon, for one—opted not to allow falconry at all.

Scrambling the situation even more was the fact that foreign nations allowed the sale of wild falcons, and one of the best-known falconers in the U.S. openly and illegally flew a gyrfalcon by showing his receipt of purchase for a Middle Eastern saker falcon, a large falcon much like a gyr in appearance.

To a bucket of confusion, add a handful of deception, stir in ignorance, and voilá! A recipe for turmoil.

Many of the first arrests by wildlife law-enforcement officers were of citizens who simply did not know the laws had been passed and that they could no longer take a wild bird as a pet. The law covered everything but common sparrows, starlings and rock doves (common pigeons). One lawman confiscated an eagle a lady had found injured years before near her Wyoming home. The bird was sitting on the back of a chair in the lady's trailer house, and the officer gingerly approached it, fearful of its big talons. There were mutes on the wall, the chair and the carpet; the lady and the eagle had become soul mates.

"No, no, no," said the lady as she watched his clumsy attempts. "You just have to pick him up like this," and she held a short, thick branch out to the eagle. The bird obediently stepped on the branch and she carried the eagle to the waiting truck and its cage.

Dave Hintze, a UDWR conservation officer, recalls his first experience with an imprinted hawk, also in the hands of a loving and qualified, but unlicensed, person in southern Utah:

This guy had the bird for two years and was taking good care of it. It was a total eyas imprint, acting just like any human youngster would act when I confiscated it, trusting and happy to go for a ride. I figured I would release the bird, but on the way to the release site, it got out of

*the box. It did not fly around in the truck. Oh, no. It climbed into my
lap and looked out over the steering wheel as I drove into the desert.
Finally I released it. I threw it in the air and it came right down. It had
been taken as an eyas and was totally unreleasable when I got it.
This is a case where the law did not fit the wildlife. The law is dogmatic,
not pragmatic. It would have been better to work with the owner so he
could become "legal" and keep the bird.*

The government men, generally an intelligent, dedicated and
altruistic bunch, began learning their raptors and turned their sights
on falconers, the largest target. Some obtained falconry licenses.
Some not only learned falconry, but went undercover. Their first
few busts of falconers resulted in little more than a handful of
feathers and no meat. The milder malefactors were charged for
practices they had carried over from preact days; like mountain men
of the 1840s, the world was changing and they were not. Meanwhile
Bill and his friends were "scamming the fish cops" whenever they
could. The wildlife lawmen eventually learned this, and unfortunately Bill's group became representative to them of all falconers.

Once, at a retirement banquet for a wildlife manager, Harry
Stiles, the USF&WS resident agent in Denver, the man who approved all our federal activities, told Stel and me flatly that "all
falconers are illegal, aren't they?" I looked off toward the salad bar,
ever aware of Shakespeare's line, "though she be little, she is fierce,"
from *A Midsummer Night's Dream,* hoping for the moment to pass.

Stellanie took considered umbrage, drawing herself up to her
full five-foot, two-inch height; the answer seemed to take forever
boiling to the surface: "Is Tom Cade illegal? Is Morlan Nelson
illegal? Is Clayton White illegal? I'm a falconer and I am not illegal
in *anything* I do." She said it slowly and precisely, looking up at Stiles
with eyes flashing, anger just below the surface. He nodded, I
relaxed, and we continued to have a good relationship with Stiles.

We found ourselves affected by the conflict between falconers
and law enforcers. Falconers could legally be allowed to take certain
birds that had been confiscated or turned in after accidents or illness,
and it was reasonable that they be allowed to take possession of a
bird we were holding, rather than take a fresh bird out of the wild.
I was stunned one morning when I heard the assistant chief of law
enforcement for the UDWR say, "I would rather see a bird dead than
with a falconer."

With people like Bill out there, and others like him, I expected
some bitterness on the part of the wildlife agents. With books being
sold like *Hard-Core Poaching,* "high tech ways to beat the game laws,"
it is no wonder they sometimes turn into misanthropes.[10]

The stage was being set for the USF&WS to execute Operation

Falcon Sting, and little did we know that we would have ringside seats. It began strangely for Stellanie and I, when our phones began to crackle and fade. I believe our telephone was tapped by the cooperating agencies in the sting for at least a couple of years prior to the actual operation. Paranoia? Perhaps. But Stellanie and I once figured out that certain comments dropped by a government person could only have resulted from hearing a conversation over our phone. Throughout this period Stellanie especially was in touch with falconers and other hawk people, and sometimes they tried to tell us things we had no need to know. We often told falconer friends and acquaintances as they launched into a suspicious-sounding story that we "didn't want to hear about it."

Our focus was on the birds in our care and as a spin-off, educating the public about birds of prey. We did our best to remain neutral in the fish cops-and-robbers escapades.

Operation Falcon Sting was carefully orchestrated by the USF&WS—up to a point. A Montana falconer and others were set up to illegally sell birds to a number of U.S. falconers, offering both peregrines and gyrfalcons taken from nests in Alaska by the wildlife service itself. After two years of this, the service coordinated a series of arrests on the same day, with the federal courts handing down counts against some fifty falconers across the country, including two men who were attempting to sell birds to Arabs. Fines were levied up to twenty-five thousand dollars, and some bad guys were corralled, among them, not surprisingly, our old friend, Dean of Disney fame.

It certainly stunned the raptor community and sent a message to falconry malefactors, but the birds also lost in the process. First, the state of Alaska's wildlife resources agency was never informed that federal agents were removing birds from their nests. Alaska state biologists became concerned about precipitous drops in nesting success.[11]

Second, more than twenty peregrines and gyrfalcons died because of inadequate care after they were retaken from falconers, and assigned to rehabilitators who apparently knew little or nothing about caring for the birds, a step apparently deemed necessary for secrecy by the USF&WS.[12]

Third, agents swept down on academic and other government projects, including the Peregrine Fund operation, and the operation of my squeaky-clean sister-in-law, Kathy Smith, who was keeping a prairie falcon, a kestrel and an eagle as a subpermittee to Stellanie. Perhaps this was to show their motives were egalitarian.

Finally, communication between hawk people disintegrated in distrust, and much shared experience was lost; we were suspected by some falconers of being in cahoots with the bust (since we were not in the sweep), and no matter how strenuously we argued our noninvolvement, some still viewed what we said as disingenuous.

I am sure the USF&WS will admit mistakes, and it needs to review its procedures and ask itself: what decisions were to the detriment of the creatures it proposed to help? Should not the individual bird come first? After all, it is a *life,* and that is very important to my mind. All the goodwill generated by wildlife biologists and managers in their attempt to communicate with the public can be dumped in a moment of law-enforcement thoughtlessness. The message the public got was that the USF&WS had done its job, but a chill still lies over the raptor community and Bill, Captain of the Scams, and others like him, danced away into the sunset, untouched by the law.

Since we took our first bird, we have had occasion to meet rehabilitators from various parts of the U.S. and Canada, and in general we greatly admired them. Most often they accepted the knowledge and help of the falconers and combined it with their own trial-and-error approaches to avian physiology and medicine, utilizing veterinary care when it was available and thoughtful.

We have also met some duds. The biggest problem in raptor rehabilitation in North America today is raptor rehabilitators, some of whom are unthinking, egotistical, undisciplined, arrogant and scornful, or all of the above (the *magalo kephali* are everywhere).

Paul Theroux says "virtuous people are uninteresting to write about," with which it would seem I wholeheartedly agree, since I've chosen to tell of those rehabilitators who give the effort a bad name. But there is also much to be learned from the mistakes of others in terms of making changes in the wildlife-management system to benefit the raptors. I believe we always operated on the principle, however difficult to live with, that we did what was best for the birds. Unfortunately many rehabilitators are people who want to take something personally *from* the hawks and eagles with which they are entrusted.

In one case a rehabilitator we will call "Betty" manifested her deep personal problems through her work with hawks. This woman first revealed a shrewish side, then unveiled great hostility and a deep-seated anger directed toward both birds and the people who worked with them. She was vocally critical of everyone in the raptor field, and a provocateur; it seemed to be her way of elevating her own sense of importance. Then she sought media coverage, which seemed to validate an ego that was otherwise shaking on a loose foundation. Small enough peccadilloes, easily overlooked, I thought at first.

Then one day Betty received a mature female California quail, perfectly tame, that would sit on her hand or shoulder. As we have discussed, all rehabbers are often entrusted with birds other than raptors. The little bird walked up to me as I sat on Betty's couch, clucking gently, curiously, taking grain from my palm.

When next I visited, I was stunned to learn she had killed this bird to feed to an owl, an act which especially disturbed me since the quail was so imprinted and totally trusting of humans that she was dependent on them entirely. There may be those who will disagree with my outrage, since a rehab person chooses to put hawks first, but I feel that there are alternatives to providing food this way. I have heard of rehabbers and others who have fed injured hawks to uninjured hawks in order to solve food problems, but I could not live with this, either.

Betty also used a truck winch to pull off the heads of two live chickens to use as food for hawks. I believe there are better ways to kill chickens, but Betty found this funny.

Betty was quick to euthanize, and lacked patience, the result of which is that many birds she listed as released we later learned from former helpers were buried in her yard or elsewhere.

We withdrew from contact and assumed the USF&WS would eventually remove her permits. No such luck.

When asked today, Betty will readily tell you she doesn't really like birds.

A couple we lovingly called the Doo-Dahs also wished to become rehabilitators. Stellanie was so hard-pressed for help that she gladly welcomed their interest, giving them a short-eared owl for a weekend test. On Monday they returned the bird with vague excuses, and after some questioning, we determined that the expense of feeding seemed to be the problem. Further questioning revealed a deeper truth: the Doo-Dahs expected to be able to treat the bird as one would a puppy, and the bird was having none of it. To their credit, they recognized that birds were not easily handled or cared for.

Wild, injured raptors do not make good pets, nor do they do well with other animals, especially dogs. Another subpermittee tried to keep a recovering kestrel with a small, nervous, noisy dog, and the result was a kestrel that was a feathered mess, constantly bating, with its beak agape, and its primaries and tail feathers broken and worn from the constant fear.

Yet another rehabber couldn't leave the birds alone; she was constantly picking at them and feeling them, causing them to bate and preventing them from healing.

Both rehabbers could not or would not hear that birds need quiet, as well as limited handling, limited medicine—"less is more."

And the bird business requires a devotion exclusively to birds, unlike some other animal fields. It's a choice you have to make for the sake of conservation.

Bird handlers may be born with "soft" ways; successful handlers and falconers have an unmistakable smoothness and gentleness in handling birds. There must be a sense of the *tao* of the bird, of its natural flow and balance, and you must move with that, not against it.

Rehabilitation began for us and many others as a personal commitment to the conservation movement, and while you can never structure a test to measure depth of commitment, many states are now requiring tests of prospective rehabilitators. Stel took her falconry test as a means of achieving some degree of credibility, and for the same reason served an apprenticeship under the aviary curator.

In addition to rigorous testing of would-be rehabbers, I strongly recommend that a conservation officer or wildlife agent be present to witness every bird release to make certain the bird is indeed being released.

A second problem for birds of prey lies in the hands of government. The vast majority of state and federal raptor workers we have met are thoughtful, gentle people genuinely committed to conservation of our natural resources. But government is inevitably going to have bad apples in the uniforms of wildlife agents. There will forever be power trips, buck-passing, inconsistencies, conflicts and red tape.

Occasionally there are serious abuses of power. Stellanie was once asked to perjure herself in a raptor case by a man who was then a federal agent. In a second instance, another empowered officer ordered certain birds to be given to certain people he personally approved of, regardless of regulations. Still another wildlife agent ordered certain birds transferred to a certain rehabilitator who was blatantly manipulating him with sex.

In one case two factions of a wildlife agency became involved in a bitter, long-running labor dispute, which destroyed morale, careers and reputations while poachers operated at will.

For those who are in the bird business for ego reasons—they like to look cool with a hawk on their fists, or because it gets them into bed with interesting people—I suggest they reassess their interest in birds of prey and invest instead in a good shrink.

Waiting to catch the wind. Stellanie Ure releasing a recovered male prairie falcon at Farmington Bay, Utah. (Photo by Jim Ure)

14
Releasing

Unextinguished laughter
shakes the skies.

—Homer

Wings were meant to fly, and our entire effort was to that end. Releasing a bird was the most joyous of events, the miracle of a healed humerus or fully feathered youngster in its first flight providing payment in sheer satisfaction.

Release day was not without its anxiety and trepidation, however, especially with those marginal hawks which had been treated, watched perhaps for months, and now were being committed to the wilderness without certainty of survival. Weeks later, months later, one of the children might say, "I wonder if Dapper Dan made it," or, "Do you think Chiquita is warm tonight?" We owed these birds the chance man had originally deprived them of.

Releasing a bird is not as simple as it sounds, since much depends on the species of bird and its ability to fly. Some fly well and need little more than being shown the door; others are trickier. We tried to match the bird with its habitat: generally open areas for buteos and falcons, and woods and riparian habitat for accipiters.

Eagles got a special federal hacking station all their own at Bear River Bay Migratory Bird Refuge, built of utility poles and graduated fencing with an open top. The sides were about twenty-five feet tall, and the station was approximately twenty-five yards wide and fifty yards long. Stellanie designed it based on conversations with Morlan Nelson and others, the theory being that an injured or sick eagle placed in such an enclosure could exercise and be well fed until it gained enough flight strength to finally clear the tall sides. The USF&WS built the station, and federal refuge workers provided food and water daily. It worked as designed to do and saw at least fifty golden and bald eagles able to clear its sides and fly free.

Some birds we hacked out in our woods, establishing a feeding station to which they could return until they were flying strongly and hunting on their own.

143

Summer days were especially busy, since spring youngsters were fledging, and it became essential to release as many as possible to make room for incoming birds.

Midmorning light dappled the patio in cottonwood patterns. On it were a table, chaise lounges, chairs—and Stel and I kicking back after a busy Saturday morning of bird chores. A brood of five kestrels I called "the Aggressives" descended like bees from the surrounding trees to the hack station set in the crotch of a tree near the house. They had been fed three times already but continued to drop by the station every few minutes "just in case" more mice or chicken had been set out. When we first released these birds, they came to the hack station and lined up in a row to be fed, just like they had been fed in their box during the previous three weeks. *Chee chee chee* they trilled as they stood at the hack station expectantly.

Cory came from the house with a red Popsicle and it was immediately seized by a kestrel which dived off the roof. He carefully peeled the little falcon off, giggling as it clung to the frozen sweet. "Don't bring a sandwich out," I said laughing. The day before, our young Rogue kestrel, a single youngster now raised and flying with the other brood, had "bound into" my corned beef sandwich.

Also flying loose were a pair of long-eared owls, Charles A. Lindberg the Lone Owl and his nestmate, Suzie. Charles and Suzie had been named by Cory, whose interest in flight has carried into his later years. They had come from a falconer who had found them in a nest destroyed by skunks in the west Utah desert.

Yet another kestrel, named Cecil, would depart this day as the ward of a youngster who had just passed his falconry test. Stellanie was writing instructions when the boy walked around the house and onto the patio:

> No more than 1/4 oz. lean beef. Feed soft chicken, 1 oz. per day. Serve complete sparrows or mice at least 1 time per week. Feed chicken necks every other day (1 each day except when whole other food available). You may feed chicken heart 3 X a week if you want, and beef heart once in a while. Dip heart in egg yolk. Apply 2 drops baby ABDEC vitamins every other day to chicken neck (can buy this at drugstore). Apply bonemeal daily to chicken neck. Feed morning and evening. Feed full crop until ready to fly on game. Then refer to your falconry manual. DO NOT ALLOW HIM TO DROP MORE THAN 1/4 OZ. IN WEIGHT.

The boy, his brand new falconry license displayed in a plastic convention tag holder on his chest (not required by law), proudly left the house with the little bird on his fist. The boy vowed he would fly the bird over Grand Canyon, and I recalled Plato: "Of all animals, the boy is the most unmanageable."

Flying birds at hack as we were had certain risks, since they could be taken by neighborhood predators, especially goshawks which we knew nested in our woods. We also had great horned owls, sharp-shinned hawks, raccoons and skunks, as well as cats and dogs which roamed the woods. We reasoned that all birds must contend with predators in the wild, and therefore they would have to do so here. With us they had the distinct advantage of three (or four or five or six) square meals a day from the hack station.

But Charles A. Lindberg the Lone Owl and his nestmate Suzie were very owly and as such were fearlessly impervious to the danger of other birds. They had been bedroom raised (he and she alternately getting the run of the room with Pepita and Strider) and then released.

The next night we heard one of the perched red-tails outside the house crying with terror and alarm. We dashed out into the yard, robes flying behind us. Suzie Owl and the red-tail were flailing around on the ground, locked in each other's clutches, and wrapped in the red-tail's leash and jesses. Suzie Owl had attacked the red-tail; her beak was snapping, she was hissing and her eyes were angry. The larger red-tail was alarmed, but more puzzled than injured.

We released Suzie again and for three days she was the proverbial loose cannon on the deck, swooping time and again on the red-tails perched in the yard. I was concerned she might go for the small kestrels. Not to worry; she was determined to catch something big.

A weekday morning: Stel was in the bathtub sipping coffee, Matthew was tunneling or panning for gold (it had to be one or the other), and Cory was further customizing his dirt bike by removing fender weight, then testing it on a dirt berm near the driveway. Then new voices as two neighbor children came by to see our boys. First there were laughter and squeals, followed by terror-filled shrieking.

Four little boys burst into the bathroom, led by Cory, with a dying Suzie Owl bleeding in his hands. She had chosen to attack Big Red, and the buteo had merely reached out, plucked her from the air with a great foot, and killed the owl by plunging its talons into her throat. Stellanie, her nose above the bubbles, sent the crying children from her bath, took a last sip of coffee, then prepared to bury Suzie; Charles was now indeed the Lone Owl.

Big Red was the most beautiful red-tail I had ever seen, with honey blond feathers that contrasted with the barless, king salmon pink of her train. Big Red was later given to Tracy Aviary as a show bird, and Stel survived, too, though with ruffled dignity.

A single sunflower grows up through the vinca major above Matt's most recent mine. Turkey, a semiderelict, semi-imprinted, cross-eyed red-tail adored by all the family for his curious and gentle manner and his honking call, lifts heavily from his perch on his "meditating branch" overlooking the yard, having been released weeks before. He does not scream like a self-respecting raptor; he bleats like a sheep-goose. I watch him flying toward the northwest until his undulating wings are lost in the tangle of the woods.

Phil Wagner arrives from the UDWR, bringing a clutch of kestrels, which Stel starts attending to. She is trying to press Cory (playing his trumpet) and Matt (wearing a homemade Godzilla costume, and trying to terrify us) into service. Here are my notes of this rather typical summer evening:

"The Stouffer's dinners are on top of the two hen pheasants in a plastic bag in the freezer," says Stel to me, for we are hungry.

The phone rings. "A lady has a small, blue-gray bird that came down her chimney. She can't catch it. What should she do?" Cory shouts.

"Wait until it tries to fly out through a closed window. It will stun itself. Then they can pick it up, take it outside, let it come to and it will fly away," yells Stel from the bedroom as she and Phil transfer the kestrels to a fresh box.

Cory talks, then there is a pause. "That's exactly what happened, Mom. They're taking the bird out now," he said, surprised at his mother's endless prescience.

The phone rings as soon as Cory has hung up. Stel (muttering) picks it up and hears a neighbor's voice: "One of your hawks is down here scaring my tennis party. It's just sitting on the light post looking down at us!"

"Oh. That's Turkey. He's an imprinted eyas red-tail. If you look at him closely, you'll see he's a genetic fluke with crossed eyes. Don't let him referee. We released him a couple of weeks ago and he just keeps hanging around the neighborhood," she added. Chitchat, good-bye.

"Cory, will you get the plastic bag with the four white mice from the freezer and put them out to thaw?" Condescending, trumpet in left hand, mice in right, Cory places the bag in a pan of warm water.

"Matt, take off the Godzilla costume and go catch some grasshoppers for the kestrels . . ."

Turkey was with us for many weeks, staying close to food, often greeting us at the door in the morning, treading around the house to see who was doing what. Stel has a wonderful photo of Cory and Turkey sitting on the "meditating branch," and I have memories of my sons walking down the lane to go to the season's first day of school, followed by a red-tailed hawk with crossed eyes which is flying along with them, tree to tree, pole to fence.

Slowly Turkey's vigor declined. One night as a storm brewed, the four of us huddled around him in the mews, sniffling, trying to provide comfort; his head kept falling on his breast, his nostrils bubbled, his breathing was labored. The next dawn, as the slushy snow of early autumn was pocked by large, wet droplets melting from the trees, I found Turkey dead in his warm, dry corner of the mews. He must have lived most of the night, for his wings and legs were still flexible and his body was warm beneath my fingers. The morning continued wet, both in and out of the house. It's funny how a handicapped bird can make its way into your heart.

Releasing birds publicly can invite problems, as we saw one evening on the news at ten:

Our old friend, Betty, appears on camera holding a red-tail she says is ready for release. She talks knowledgeably about the bird, then flings it skyward. The bird pumps valiantly but falls to the ground a hundred yards away, in full view of the camera. Excuses and rationalizations are offered, and the show is saved by an astute newsman who explains that even in the wild, some birds don't make it. Betty appears to be raging in the background as she pursues the running bird.

There was very nearly a repeat of the incident when a friend at Brigham Young University, doing a study of goshawks and other accipiters on the property of Robert Redford at nearby Sundance, volunteered to find an eagle to release at a special environmental program Redford was hosting. Stel had a large female eagle that had been healing from gunshot wounds for weeks, but she warned our friend the bird might not be a good release. It was *so* important, said our friend, and with reluctance Stel agreed.

We drove to Sundance with the eagle, where our friend took her from Stel and grandly presented her to Redford, giving him and his group a brief history of the bird. The cameras were there of course, and Stellanie and I hung back on the edge of the crowd, holding our breaths.

Up went the eagle. Being a wise old bird, she immediately saw a downhill flight path through the aspen. We could see the heaviness of her injured wing, but the old girl slowly beat her way down the slope, gained a little altitude, and dropped from view over a ridge. Everyone applauded so no one could hear the sighs of relief from Stel and me. I hope the bird gained strength in her new freedom; she was smart enough that even without perfect flight abilities, she might have made it.

Often there are moments to be savored as a bird is given back to

147

the sky: a prairie falcon that leaves the fist and flies swiftly and surely across the dusky green-violet of the west desert sage lands; an eagle seeming to race a military fighter jet as it flies to freedom in Antelope Valley, not far from the air force gunnery range; a sharp-shin that slips immediately into the comfort of the cottonwood and willow woods, to be seen the next day in hot pursuit of a cackling flicker; a rough-leg with a perfectly healed wing fracture liquidly stroking his way north to the waiting tundra.

Such a moment came when Donald Dale Jackson, on assignment from *Sports Illustrated,* visited our project and immersed himself in raptor lore and legend for a lengthy article on the state of American raptors, particularly the peregrine. As Don followed Stel through her daily bird chores, he asked if she might have a bird to release. It happened that a marsh hawk was as ready as it would ever be, and the two of them traveled to the area near the mouth of Big Cottonwood Canyon where Rodriguez Carter had been released, a place we found convenient, and unpopulated, and that offered a view of the entire valley—ostensibly so a hawk could tune in to its cosmic navigation system and get its bearings. In fact it was just a breathtaking view of Salt Lake Valley, the lake stretching clear to the north horizon, with tan island-dumplings floating in its broth; the Oquirrhs and Wasatch Mountains marching south in white and purple robes.

Stel opened the box with a fear and trepidation generated only by the presence of the New York press; the marshie turned her head, looked out, then bolted from the box as if shot from a cannon, quickly catching the wind in her tippy harrier way, caught like a leaf in a dust devil, whirling ever higher in spirals that grew looser with each turn, until at last she had mounted up against towering Mount Olympus, to be lost against its five-hundred-million-year-old quartzites, then to reappear as a pepper grain against the great, white, puff-pastry cumulus piled over the Wasatch.

"That was *something,*" Don exclaimed. The resulting article was very complimentary, and was the forerunner to pieces done on Stel and the birds by magazines, newspapers and television across the country. Stel was even named "Woman of the Month" by the *Ladies' Home Journal.* "They've just discovered a small woman with a big eagle," she sniffed, dismissing any contribution she might be making.

Tufter, our long-time great-horned owl guest, assists in manuscript revisions.
(Photo by Stellanie Ure)

15
WHERE ARE THEY NOW?

*When to the sessions of sweet
silent thought I summon up
remembrances of things past*
—SHAKESPEARE

Were there contributions made by our work? Or was it, as some claimed, futile and counter to nature's wishes for the birds?

I think the biggest contribution may have been to Stellanie, myself, Cory and Matt, for by *acting* on our beliefs, we took responsibility and in doing so were set free—free to take control of processes we thought lay only in the hands of politicians. The problems of the environment may be beyond our power to solve, but because we take responsibility where we can, we are no longer helpless, as an unsigned *New Yorker* piece exhorted recently.

We helped many birds, but we also influenced many people, and I believe that is where the benefit may lie. We gave the public access to providing help in the only way they could—by bringing birds to us. The public also became more aware of birds of prey, of the way the earth works, and of the importance of all life in its web. People living in cities have often become oblivious to the natural world, forgetting that beef comes from cattle, water from rain, wheat from vegetation, milk from cows and Kentucky Fried regular and crispy from birds. Everything starts with the earth and its parts.

After several years in our project, I realized that I was meeting people who were anxious to share their nature experiences. Total strangers called to tell us of a hummingbird that had become a backyard friend, of a hawk that regularly sat on a pole at their favorite fishing spot, or the certain sighting of a peregrine falcon eating seed from their neighbor's bird feeder. The point is: people in my area became more sensitized to hawks in particular and nature in general.

During these years there was much press exposure, and we took part in special events with business and institutions of all kinds in an attempt to raise the consciousness of the public, very important in our community where dominion of the earth has been the rule since Utah was settled by Anglos in 1847.

There were some other interesting contributions, especially research published by Stellanie and Dr. Jack Taylor on their discovery of leucocytozoans in birds of prey. Stel first noticed that blood research on darker-colored birds of many species almost always produced leucocytozoans. This needs more research, but it may be helpful for adaptive reasons.

Our family was also the first to receive and identify a black hawk in Utah (brought to us from southern Utah) and a red-shouldered hawk (rare here, found near Grantsville, identified by Cory, written up by Clayton White).

There were a thousand dreams, a thousand conversations, a thousand ideas—some of the latter reaching fruition through the efforts of others.

The falconers benefited through Stel's knowledge of both physiology and behavior, but the truth is she was doing it for the birds always, for after all these years, we are totally certain each bird has its own personality and its own soul, its unique spark of life as important as mine or yours.

Birds of prey are barometers of the environment and as such deserve scientific study. But they are most important for our mental health, works of art filling us with awe, beauty and wonder, as much, I think, as Michelangelo or Monet. "All art is but imitation of nature," Seneca said. Birds are an art created by fifty million years of selection, shaped by powers higher than humanity can adequately understand.

The human race, for all its intellectualism, is limited to what can be derived from the senses. Just as surely as birds can't talk like humans, neither can humans communicate like birds. And birds can *fly* besides. People's arrogance and homocentricity have led them to overvalue their role in this world. Humans must now act responsibly toward the earth, or it is the human species which will pay the ultimate price.

Humanity may take some creatures with it if it populates itself into a diseased or starved (or nuclear) extinction, but I will bet that when the dust settles and the corpses have been strewn by the coyotes (certain survivors), a kestrel will sit on a tattered, impotent power pole aside the still wreckage of a "Mad Max" freeway, bobbing his tail, and calling *chee chee chee*. Strangely I find that comforting.

I speak for Stel when I say we are exhausted and staggering under the work—and load—of the ethical questions we have shouldered since we got into the business.

I can no longer look a bird in the eye with any notion of killing for sport. Predation is natural, and I enjoy a good steak or coq au vin as much as the next person, for I realize that in order for me to eat, something must die. But I have been involved so deeply in life-and-death decisions these last years; from the death of mice to the euthanizing of hawks, owls and eagles too sick to make it any longer.

Sometimes Stel was able to get a UDWR worker or a veterinarian to euthanize a bird. Often it fell to me, and it is difficult to look a redtail in the eye as a euthanizing needle is inserted under its rib cage. It is just as difficult to hold the bird being euthanized, feeling the warmth of its feet, the thumping of its heart, the sweet, musty warmth of its breath. Then suddenly the gaping beak, the distended tongue, a shudder and tightening, the relaxation of death and the drooping head.

It is difficult to place a flailing golden eagle in a box, place the box in a plastic bag, then run the exhaust hose from the car into the plastic bag. The bird *knows*.

Who is to live and who is to die? That was a question that haunted us. Can you, golden eagle, make it if that bone heals? If you live another month, maybe you'll regain your strength from that poison; maybe you won't though, and you are eating a rat every day, a rat that a survivor may need. We need your food and your mews space if you are not going to make it.

And you, prairie falcon: you are a perfectly healthy bird, but you will never fly again. Since you are cosmetically okay, perhaps a zoo will take you. Better that than death, I suppose, but sometimes not much, since many zoos are demeaning, analogous to slavery in the nineteenth century. (Zoos in Asia and Third World countries often provide only the most wretched of conditions.) When will people realize creatures are sentient and feeling?

Can we give you to a person who would simply like to keep a bird? The law says no, yet that person can buy a gun and a license and go kill a bird. Wouldn't it be good to have a system of providing unreleasable birds to the public? Too difficult to police, say the law-enforcement people.

And what about government-funded rehabilitation centers? No money, say the wildlife agencies. No wonder the public is schizoid, angry at their wildlife agencies on one hand, yet sympathetic on the other.

In the beginning I faced these inequities matter-of-factly. Today I agonize and must turn to the Great Hawk for strength and courage.

I planned to spend my usual Saturday afield at Bear River Bay, primarily to see birds, but needing an excuse to clean out my locker at the Duckville Gun Club. My membership in the venerable old club had been sold, and Great Salt Lake's rising waters promised to inundate the clubhouse within weeks. Stel and the kids decided to come along and after the usual organizational shouts and mutterings, the show was on the road.

Soon we turned down the main street of Brigham City, wondering aloud what the town fathers would do about the big sign crossing over the street, proclaiming it Gateway to the World's Greatest Game Bird Refuge. For sixty years Great Salt Lake had sloshed around pretty much at the same level in the basin, but lately it was rising dramatically, swamping highways, industrial lowlands and farms. About to go were the state and federal wetlands developed for migratory birds; after that vast tracts of residential subdivisions would go under. Utahns were getting a demonstration that they could not take this earth for granted, and Mother Nature was throwing spitballs.

We buzzed over the cattle guards past the little egrets feeding in the shallows. Red-winged blackbirds were thick in the cattails, singing their spring *okalee*. Dense columns of gnats formed alongside the road, looking like pillars of smoke rising from underground fires. The water was very high, and old fence lines were drowning, flats where I once hunted geese were a foot deep in brackish water, and huge carp showed their backs where they spawned, leaving swirls of mud as they dashed from the thump of tires. Bow hunters stalked them from the roadside.

Driving the fourteen miles from town to Duckville was a new experience, with water from horizon to horizon. A mile from Duckville, the USF&WS personnel were packing everything from the laboratory at refuge headquarters, where landmark botulism research had taken place, a reminder of the great drought years of the 1930s. The hacking station built for our birds at the refuge headquarters was to be dismantled within a week, then shipped to another site after being given to the state.

We decided to drive around the refuge before stopping at the club. The imminent flooding was undeniable; water was beginning to spill over the dikes at a dozen places on the refuge perimeter. The big resting ponds were filled to capacity and erosive cuts had appeared, through which flowed a rush of briny water from Great Salt Lake. No one would speculate on when or if the refuge could open again.

As we drove slowly around Unit Two, the tires of the car sizzled through shallow sheets of water sloshing into the refuge from cresting lake waves. Baby Canada geese were already out, steaming behind the adults like flotillas of fuzzy bathtub warships. Soon even the geese would abandon the refuge for higher ground.

As we neared the corner observation post at the south end of the unit, we stopped. These elevated steel decks had been built only a few years before, and already there was a bulky stick nest on this one, just below the platform. "Raven," I noted, more to myself than anyone else.

We drew closer and I stopped, thinking to climb up to the platform. A raven's head popped up over the top of the stick bundle. "Chiquita! Chiquita!" shouted the boys.

The raven looked down without fear, turning its head from side to side. *QUORK!* It was a gentle sound of curiosity.

Matt and Cory are certain it was our Chiquita. Stel is certain it was Chiquita. A wild raven would have taken flight, so I am certain it was Chiquita. If only my attempts to teach her to say "nevermore" had been successful, we'd have known positively.

It was a happy moment, and we did not climb the deck for fear of disturbing eggs or babies. When we left the refuge, we told one of the workers that our old raven was nesting on the overlook, and could he put up a sign or gate to keep her from being disturbed?

A few minutes later I was flooded with memories as I walked into the locker room at Duckville. I had been a member of the club for fifteen years.

Bereft of tables, the dining room echoed my footsteps, as well as the ghost sounds of tinkling glasses and fireside conversation. The furnaces had been removed, the fireplace was cleaned out, the big ice maker in the bar was gone, the furniture had been stowed in the attic.

I looked out across the Bear River and remembered nights of autumn alive with the sound of thousands of migrating tundra swans. I could almost feel the rush of cold air as the airboat raced across the shallows toward the tamarisk mirages on the horizon, the raw wind blasting my face and jamming my nostrils as the boat streaked south beneath great flocks of high-flying pintails and green-winged teal.

A photo of a friend, now dead, was tacked to the bulletin board, its corners slowly turning upward. I indulged myself a last reverie as I looked into one of the spartan bedrooms: weekends at the club with Stel and the kids and Steve Chindgren and BBG when we would hawk the golden fields of the nearby farmlands.

I turned away from the emotions that tugged like a boat in the wind and rummaged in my locker. The decoys would go to Cory; he may yet do some hunting. A friend wanted to buy my shotguns. I could use the waders for fishing. The bulky Jones coat would snuggle me on January birding days, and the gloves were wonderfully warm for skiing, snow shoveling or hiking. I left three boxes of shotgun shells on the locker-room table. I would no longer be hunting, and someone would take them.

We had released a lot of birds here. Eagles had flown free; so had marsh hawks, prairie falcons, kestrels, barn owls and one rascal raven. Godspeed Chiquita ... Lady ... Flam ... Muscles ... Sundrop ... 76 ... Silvio ... Dapper Dan and Dixie ... Sherman ... Roommate ... and all the unnamed birds in our notes and records. Godspeed.

Strider lives under the bed. Pepita sits silent as stone on a faucet handle and sometimes we cannot find him when he is right in front of us. Baby has mothered four broods of eaglets, Cory has just made Cottonwood High School Marching Band, and there are peregrines now nesting in downtown Salt Lake City. Oh yes: Matthew actually found gold in Big Cottonwood Creek almost in our backyard, and the UDWR confirmed there is a pair of breeding bald eagles in Westwater Canyon, the first in Utah. "Let the great world spin forever down the ringing grooves of change," as Tennyson said.

Epilogue

From 1973 until 1986 we handled about three thousand birds in our project, first called the Utah Raptor Rehab Group, and later the Raptor Society. At last calculation we had a release rate of 51 percent, with another 26 percent going to falconers, zoos, aviaries, researchers or other rehabilitators. About 21 percent were euthanized.

We had in temporary possession every indigenous western raptor but three: gyrfalcons, *Falco rusticolus;* merlins, *Falco columbarius,* and turkey vultures, *Cathartes aura.*

We cannot guess at our success rate, for only seven bands have been received from the more than seven hundred birds that Stellanie banded and released. All were returned from Utah, but far enough from our release sites to indicate survival for some time after release. We hope that someday funds may be available for more sophisticated tracking and study.

FOOTNOTES

Chapter Four: First Birds

1. Descriptions, habitat, food, nesting and other information in this book come from a variety of sources. Foremost among them is *Life Histories of North American Birds of Prey*, by Arthur Cleveland Bent, reprinted by Dover Publications, Inc., New York City. The copies I have were copyrighted in 1961, but I know the book is still available at bookstores. These life histories were originally published in 1937 as *Smithsonian Institution United States National Museum Bulletin 167*, and in 1938 as *Bulletin 170*. This series of bulletins was first published in 1875, and consists of monographs of large zoological groups and other systematic treatises, faunal works, reports of expeditions, catalogues, special collections, etc. Bent compiled this series, and it is an essential part of any raptor library. It sometimes shocks the contemporary reader: "I dispatched the adults with my shotgun and took the eggs for my collection." Bird watching was done over the sights of a Winchester until only recently.

Other important raptor reference books the reader may wish to consult include *Eagles, Hawks and Falcons of the World*, by Leslie Brown and Dean Amadon, 1989 edition by The Wellfleet Press, Secaucus, New Jersey. Raptor books and catalogues of raptor books are available from sources including Buteo Books, a raptor book specialist in Vermillion, South Dakota 57069, and from the Peregrine Fund, World Center for Birds of Prey, 5666 W. Flying Hawk Lane, Boise, Idaho 83709.

Of the falconry books, I would recommend the time-honored classic, *The Art of Falconry, Being De Arte Venandi cum Avibus*, of Frederick II of Hohenstaufen, translated and edited by Casey A. Wood and F. Marjorie Fyfe, Stanford University Press, Stanford, California, first published in 1943. The most complete contemporary book of falconry for the U.S. and Canada is probably *North American Falconry and Hunting Hawks*, by Frank Lyman Beebe and Harold Melvin Webster, published by North American Falconry and Hunting Hawks, P. O. Box 1484, Denver, Colorado, 80201, copyright 1985.

In addition to these and many other books, some of the information in this book has been collected from individual papers by raptor biologists on a variety of birds and subjects.

2. Bent, pp. 295, 348.

3. Ibid.

4. Ibid. One great horned owl banded in Iowa lived thirteen-to-

fourteen years before it was shot near its place of banding. One study reported that of 374 owls banded in the U.S., shooting by hunters was the cause of death for 52 percent. (This information comes from the *Audubon Society Encyclopedia of North American Birds*, John K. Terres, editor. New York: Alfred A. Knopf, 1982.)

Chapter Seven: Householding with Hawks
    5. Bent, pp. 384, 396.
    6. Ibid.
    7. Ibid, p. 164.

Chapter Twelve: Contributions of Falconry
    8. Bent, p. 60.
    9. Ibid, p. 45.

Chapter Thirteen: The Heat of Conflict
    10. *Hard-Core Poaching*, by Ragnar Benson, Paladin Press, Boulder, Colorado, 1986.
    11. Personal commentary by Ron Clarke, an Alaskan falconer and member of the staff of the governor of Alaska.
    12. Paul McKay, "Criminal Justice," in "A Special Report on Operation Falcon," *The Whig Standard Magazine* (Oct. 31, 1987): 1-32.

GLOSSARY

I have bought me a hawk and a hood, and bells and all, and lack nothing but a book to keep it by.

—BEN JOHNSON, 1598

This glossary is compiled from the extensive terms, words and expressions peculiar to falconry, most of which are listed in the Casey A. Wood and F. Marjorie Fyfe translation of *De Arte Venandi cum Avibus (The Art of Falconry)*, by Frederick II of Hohenstaufen, completed about 1248, and published by Stanford University Press in 1943. The original includes many Latin terms and vulgate phrases, whose translations created consternation even for Frederick. The terms in this glossary are still used by falconers and raptor scientists and specialists as we enter the twenty-first century.

Astringer (n.) One who owns and flies short-winged hawks (accipiters, including goshawks, Cooper's hawks, sharp-shinned hawks). Also austringer or ostringer.

Bagged quarry (n.) Live pigeons or other birds or animals kept for training hawks.

Barbel (n.) One of the small processes fringing the barbs of a feather. Also barbule.

Bate (v.) To spring from a perch or the fist in an attempt to fly away.

Beam feathers (n.) The long pinions of the wings; the primaries.

Bell (n.) Hawk's bell, or nola, also campanella. A small bell attached to the hawk's feet or around its neck. Its sound may be used to locate the bird in flight or when in heavy cover.

Bewits (n.) The leather straps attached to the hawk's feet to carry the bells and to hold the bird on the fist.

Bind (v.) To seize and fasten on the quarry, as in "she bound into the duck."

Block, Block perch (n.) An inverted pyramid, truncated cone, or cylinder of wood or stone, commonly encircled by a ring or other device and provided with an arrangement for attaching the leash, on which the hawk is placed to weather, feed and bathe.

Bow net (n.) Device for catching hawks; a net stretched over a metal half-hoop and worked by a cord.

Bow perch (n.) A perch in the shape of a half circle, with the ends sunk in the ground or attached to a metal plate.

Brancher (n.) A fledgling that is able to hop from branch to branch near the nest. Also bowet, or bowiser.

Brayle, Brail (n.) Leather thong with a slit in it to put about and confine a hawk's wing. Also corrigiola.

160

Cast of hawks (n.) A pair of hawks.

Cere (n.) The smooth, waxlike integument (cera) at the base of the upper mandibles. The yellow patch between beak and eyes.

Coping (v.) Paring or dulling the sharp points of the hawk's beak or talons. The wild bird accomplishes it by rubbing them on a rock or other hard surface.

Crab (v.) To fight (said of two falcons or two birds of prey).

Creance (n.) Fine cord or line attached to the hawk's leash when it is first flown to the lure.

Crop (n.) Upper portion of the gullet where the food first lodges after swallowing.

Deck feathers (n.) The two central feathers of the tail.

Droppings (n.) The excrement of the falcon vented as it drops, instead of being ejected, or sliced, straight backward. Falcons and owls drop, eagles and accipiters slice.

Enter a hawk (v.) To fly for a first kill in training. To make the hawk acquainted with the type of prey it is to be hunting.

Eyas (n.) Young hawk taken from the nest. Also eyass, eyess.

Eyrie (n.) Hawk's nesting place. Also eyre, eyry, aiery, or ayre.

Falcon (n.) In many English treatises referring to the female peregrine in particular, but applied as a rule to the female of all long-winged hawks.

Falcon gentle (n.) Male of the species, generally the tercel.

Falconer's glove (n.) A gauntlet of heavy leather to protect (from talons and beak) the hand and wrist carrying the bird.

Feak, Feake (v.) To wipe the beak on the perch after feeding.

Flags (n.) Secondaries, wing feathers; also plumage next to the principal wing feathers.

Flight feathers (n.) The pinions of the wing.

Fly on (v.) Choice of prey for the hawk, as in "What do you fly her on?"

Frounce (n.) Canker or sore in the throat and mouth.

Gorge (v.) To eat to repletion.

Hack (n.) Place, usually out-of-doors, where the hawk is fed and is allowed liberty. A hack board is set up, and food is placed on this for the bird to return to and eat.

Hood (n.) Leather head covering for blinding the hawk, first introduced from the Orient to Europe by Frederick II.

Hunger traces (n.) Feathers showing traces of starvation or improper feeding.

Imp (v.) To repair a broken pinion by substituting a metal shaft or needle and part of another feather. In the twentieth century, imping was made easier by the advent of plastics and Super Glue. (A major feather may be replaced by using even the feather of another bird species. There is one legendary red-tailed hawk released and seen flying with the violet-blue primary of a hyacinth macaw—the result of imping. Local birders were astounded.) Falconers usually try to keep a number of moulted feathers around for imping purposes.

Jack (n.) The male hawk.

Jerkin (n.) The male of the gyrfalcon.

Leash (n.) A narrow leather thong attached to the jesses and perch; it may be wrapped around the hand to hold fast a captive bird.

Lime (n.) Birdlime. An extremely adhesive, viscid excretion of the holly, mistletoe, or breadfruit, so called because twigs smeared with it were and still are used to capture small birds.

Lure (n.) A weighted, leather device to which are attached a couple of pigeon or other wings. Garnished with meat, it serves, when swung about the falconer's head, to attract the free-flying bird to the lure and back to his fist. Also a verb: to lure the bird back.

Make into (v.) The act of approaching the hawk as it sits on the kill.

Malers (n.) The dark feathers masking the eyes of falcons, especially peregrines.

Man (v.) To tame or to get the falcon accustomed to the presence of human beings.

Mantle (v.) To stretch one wing after another, then the legs, and then the other body members. In modern usage this is a position taken by the hawk over its quarry after making the kill: wings extended, neck arching downward, the quarry firmly clutched. Often accompanied by a sharp, piercing cry.

Mews (n.) The house in which hawks reside.

Moult (v.) To shed old feathers one by one and thus acquire new plumage.

Mutes (n.) Bird excrement.

Nares (n.) Nasal cavities, nostrils.

Overhawked (adj.) Having or attempting to keep too many hawks.

Passage hawk (n.) A falcon (traditionally a peregrine) captured during migration.

Pitch (n.) The altitude reached by the falcon on ringing up.

Plume (v.) To strip or pluck the feathers off the quarry.

Pounces (n.) Talons.

Rake away (v.) To take off, to fly wide or avoid the quarry, apparently for exercise or to amuse oneself.

Rangle (n.) Small pebbles given to the hawk to aid digestion. It will take them voluntarily. The equivalent of *grit* in poultry and pigeons.

Ring up (v.) To rise in spirals high into the air; to mount or soar.

Sails (n.) The wings of a hawk.

Screamer (n.) A young hawk in training; an eyas that has developed the vice of screaming.

Sharp set (adj.) Very hungry.

Slicing (v.) (See *mute*.) Excreting a considerable distance.

Slip (v.) To cast off or fly the hawk.

Stoop (n.) The lightninglike plunge of the falcon on the quarry beneath it.

Swivel (n.) Device for preventing twisting or entanglement of hawks' jesses and leashes. Also used for this purpose were *tyrrits* and *varvels*.

Tercel (n.) The male of any variety of hawk. Probably derived from the usual occurrence that the male is one-third smaller than the female. Also spelled *tiercel, tassel, tarsell.*

Train (n.) The tail of the hawk.

Venari cum Avibus (Latin v.) To hawk.

Wait on (v.) To hover and wait for the attack, said of the falcon circling the falconer and waiting for the quarry to be flushed.

Weather (v.) To place the hawk outdoors on a block.

Yarik (adj.) Oriental term describing a hawk fit and eager to hunt. Accipiters especially are said to be in a yarik state when they seem almost frantic to kill.